OVER
THE BAR

A Personal Relationship with the GAA

BREANDÁN Ó hEITHIR (1930-1990) was one of the best-loved observers and commentators on Irish life. From Inishmore in the Aran Islands, he dropped out of university and became a salesman for Irish-language books and a promoter of the Irish language. He moved to journalism in the 1950s and became an editor at the *Irish Press* in 1957. He joined RTE in 1963 to work as a sports commentator, reporter and scriptwriter. A nephew of the writer Liam O'Flaherty, his own novel *Lig Sinn I gCathú* (1976) was the first fiction in Irish to top the bestseller list and met with widespread critical and popular acclaim.

OVER
THE BAR

A Personal Relationship with the GAA

Breandán Ó hEithir

The Collins Press

This edition published in 2005 by
The Collins Press
West Link Park
Doughcloyne
Wilton
Cork

First published in 1984 by Ward River Press

British Library Cataloguing in Publication Data

Ó hEithir, Breandán, 1930-
    Over the bar : a personal relationship with the GAA
    1. Gaelic Athletic Association 2. Gaelic games - Ireland -
    Anecdotes
    I. Title
    796'.060415

ISBN 1903464749

Printed in Ireland by Colour Books

Cover: Oldtown Design
Cover photograph: Wexford team relaxing during the Minor Final
prior to their participation in the All-Ireland Hurling Final,
Croke Park, 1955, © Ibar Carty, P.A. Crane Collection

ACKNOWLEDGEMENTS

For kind permission to reprint copyright material, acknowledgement is due to The Mercier Press Ltd. for extracts from *Dublin Made Me* by C.S. Andrews; to Sáirséal Ó Marcaigh for lines from *Briseadh na Teorann* by Earnán de Blaghd; to Frederick Muller Ltd. for extracts from *Michael Joe* by William Cotter Murray; to Routledge & Kegan Paul Ltd. for extracts from *The Shaping of Modern Ireland* edited by Conor Cruise O'Brien; to the author and Wolfhound Press for lines from "The Fanatic" in *The Pedlar's Revenge and Other Stories* by Liam O'Flaherty, available in paperback under the title *Short Stories by Liam O'Flaherty*.

Thanks also to the staffs of the National Library, RTE Library, the County Library in Tralee and Ms Eileen Cook of Trinity College Library; to Mick Dunne of RTE for the use of his comprehensive records; to Declan Brennan, Séamus Conaty, Aindreas Ó Gallchóir and Mícheál Ó Muircheartaigh for allowing me to pick their brains and sift their memories; to Ruairí and Catherine for typing and correcting; to Mary and Bernard Laughlin, custodians of the Tyrone Guthrie Centre in Annaghmakerrig, for food and shelter; and to the First National Building Society for the use of the house where the rest of it was written.

For Liam O'Flaherty,
who died shortly after it was completed,
in memory of many happy days in Croke Park

One wet and stormy night during the last war, a delegate from a rural club in County Meath got up on his bicycle to travel the thirteen Irish miles to a County Board meeting in Navan. When he arrived he was soaked through to the skin and when he sat at the table the water from his clothes flowed over it to such an extent that it was a hindrance to the conduct of business.

Then, the Holy Ghost descended on the Vice-Chairman and he proposed that the meeting should adjourn for twenty minutes. When the motion was carried he took the saturated delegate to Spicer's Bakery, nearby, and placing him carefully at the mouth of one of the ovens, turned him and twisted him until he was baked as dry as a bone.

The meeting was then resumed, and when all the business had been attended to the delegate got up on his bicycle and travelled the thirteen miles home again in the lashing rain.

It is to this anonymous delegate that this account of a personal and not always easy relationship with the Gaelic Athletic Association is dedicated. Without him and the many thousands like him, in the parishes of Ireland down the years, the GAA would not have survived.

Long may it continue to entertain, exasperate and invigorate.

1

The Gaelic Athletic Association had no presence on the island where I grew up. The Catholic Church and the Fianna Fáil party were the only popular organisations of note in Inis Mór, largest of the three Aran Islands. Fine Gael had a more discreet presence, choosing to manifest itself through the blood and marriage relations of Máirtín Mór McDonough, who was a TD for Galway in the early thirties.

Therefore, while religion and politics played an important part in the life of the island, organised sport and culture played no part at all. The only Gaelic sportsmen whose names were widely known, to the best of my recollection, were Mick Mackey and Big Tom O'Reilly. The Royal National Lifeboat Institution, which operated the Galway Bay lifeboat in Kilronan harbour from its headquarters in London, was closer to us than any national organisation.

Radio broadcasting was very much in its infancy then. Sets were few and far between and expensive to run, needing high tension (dry) batteries and low tension (wet) batteries which had to be sent to Galway for charging. In summer we got the daily papers regularly twice a week. In winter, when the old *Dún Aengus* sailed "weather and other circumstances permitting" (as the sailing card had it) we were often cut off for a week or more and the papers arrived in bundles.

Nature had seen to it that the level grass-covered land, necessary for the playing of hurling and football, was scarce and far too valuable to be trampled and torn by the boots of vigorous young men. To add to that fundamental problem, a lot of what good land did exist was broken up into small pastures surrounded by high walls of sharp limestone.

In the whole island there were about five or six fields suitable for a game of football but their owners guarded them jealously. One of them had a shotgun and a reputation for ferocity that was deterrent enough without any additional armament. He was left severely alone. The others had ears like does and eyes like hawks and the occasional attempts to steal a march on their property ended with landowner in hot pursuit of owner of football.

Indeed, footballs were rare enough objects in those days and between hobnailed boots and spiky limestone walls, had short life-spans. One that I got as a present, when I was nine, lasted about two weeks before its cover gave up the unequal struggle and fell apart at the seams. We then returned to our own traditional sports and pastimes which, in retrospect, remind me of the list of outlandish pastimes given by Dr Croke in his letter accepting the invitation to be the first patron of the GAA. In Inis Mór we could have added a few of our own. So full was our calendar that we only became aware of the major national game whenever a football appeared as a distraction in our midst.

We had a form of rounders called *bál ard*, or high ball, played between teams chosen on the spot by the two appointed captains. As it only called for two bases it could be played along a road, on the strand at low tide, or in a fairly small field. The batting side was dismissed when one of its number was hit with the ball, while running between the bases, by one of the fielding team. This game had the advantage that it could be played by boys and girls up to the age when girls lost interest in such activities; which was the age when boys' interest in them took on a new aspect.

In winter we played a form of hurling called *camóga* (crooked sticks), closer to hockey than to hurling as it was played on the ground with hazel, holly or blackthorn sticks cut at the crook near the root. It was usually played with a big sponge ball, along a stretch of road and between two goals marked with stones. Handling the ball was forbidden and any number of players could take part, the "pitch" being lengthened as the numbers increased. The absence of a referee, as there were no rules governing foul play, called for a certain hardiness as barked knuckles and bruised legs were frequent. Still, I do not recall one serious injury or the deliberate use of the stick on an opponent. If disputes occurred we had ways of settling them, as we shall see.

Other pastimes came and went with the seasons. Suddenly, and without pre-arrangement, everyone took to spinning homemade wooden tops of all shapes and sizes. The air buzzed as they were lashed along the road, or on the flat limestone flags, with whips. Just as suddenly the tops were put aside for it was pitch and toss time. This was played at school, where gambling was forbidden, with buttons and with our precious halfpence when we were admitted to the "schools" run by older boys.

There was also a game called *cead*, played with a round piece of wood, usually a three-inch section of broom handle sharpened at both ends. It was placed in a heel-mark in dry ground, tipped delicately with a long stick causing it to spring into the air and then hit for distance. Distance was measured by steps, the length of which was decided by the accumulated distance covered in an agreed number of hits.

We also wrestled (the best of three falls), cast stone boulders for distance, kidnapped puck goats during the mating season and searched for birds' nests.

Then there were the fist fights. These were no casual brawls but the result of a challenge issued during an argument, or an attempt to establish the supremacy of one pugilist over another. The use of the head or boot, gouging, or any attempt to use an instrument other than the fists were strictly forbidden and anyone who transgressed was branded a coward and lost all respect. The fight ended when one party admitted defeat but occasionally a draw was declared when the fighters were neither fit to continue nor willing to submit.

My own direct involvement in these contests came to an early end when a "soft" nose that bled far too easily cast me in the role of go-between, holder of my man's jacket and satchel and objector to foul play. Sometimes, like cockfighters, our contest was interrupted and we had to take to our heels and try to find a more secluded pitch for the confrontation.

Many years later, when I was a student in UCG and bidding farewell to a school friend who was on his way to America, one of these abandoned fights led to a hilarious incident. Among the large crowd gathered in the Four Corners Bar, across the street from Lynch's Castle, was a contemporary from the western side of the island, who had been my friend's opponent in a fight that had taken place on St Stephen's Day, ten years previously. The contest had come to an abrupt end when the curate arrived on his bike, full of pacifism, and sent us all scurrying for cover.

Maudlin reminiscence led to conjecture about the possible outcome and that in turn led to a new awakening of interest and a renewal of the original challenge. It was all very simple and even friendly and it was only when older and wiser men who were present realised that this fight was to take place outside, there and then, that they took matters in hand. They succeeded in explaining to the combatants that citizens of the city centre and the Garda Síochána were likely to get a very wrong impression of what was intended as a sentimental re-match. Peace was restored, hands were clasped several times over and many pints were consumed. Life was beautifully simple in those days.

And let me not forget stone-throwing, hardly a remarkable activity in a place where stones of all sizes abounded and when one's instinctive reaction, when attempting to discipline or intimidate an unruly animal, was to pick up a stone and let fly. But when I speak of stone-throwing I mean organised contests between groups from different villages; these were rightly regarded with horror and could only be practised far away from the eyes of our guardians.

They were usually organised for a Sunday evening, far from the villages, and at a time when few people were likely to be in that part of the island. Victory was achieved when one side was scattered by fusillades of well-directed stones, gathered by helpers and thrown by the marksmen.

It was a miracle that no one was seriously injured in any of the contests I took part in. Even now I can recollect with horror how we dodged the whistling stones, at the last minute, while advancing on the run to launch a counter-attack. I feel that neither Dr Croke nor Michael Cusack would have approved, although the man from the Burren would at least have understood the temptation.

A very old man in the village of Eochaill, who had gone to America in a sailing ship and without a word of English, once told me that to while away Sunday afternoons in Boston — the only free day in their working week — men from Aran and Connemara went to a piece of deserted common and engaged in a stone-throwing contest. They divided into two teams, usually Aran Islanders against Connemaramen, and when they tired they went to the saloon for their modest weekly drink.

Small wonder then that one of the commonest local jokes concerned a young soldier on sentry duty for the First Irish-speaking Battalion at Renmore Barracks in Galway. Having twice, and to no avail, challenged an intruder in the darkness, he shouted in Irish, "You son of a bitch, you'd soon stop if I had a stone!" I noticed, however, that when the story was told in Connemara the soldier came from Inis Mór while in Inis Mór he was clearly identified as a native of Leitir Móir.

My social life on the island and particularly my involvement in the more hazardous pastimes (such as climbing down cliffs in search of birds' eggs, or taking currachs that had come over from Inis Meáin and Inis Oírr for spins in the harbour, without the consent of their owners) was regulated and restricted by the fact that my parents taught in the village school. At an early age I developed a keen sense of self-preservation, as well as the long, accurate memory without which the liar has small chance of survival. For if I were caught misbehaving I was doubly punished: by my father at home and then again at school with my companions in mischief. Being a fair man, and to show that there was no favouritism, he never counted carefully when it came to my turn.

My companions also realised that I could be something of a Jonah. People were quicker to report witnessed misdemeanours to the teacher if they were able to mention, in passing, that they might have said nothing but for their regard for his own son's good health and life expectancy.

It is as well to explain that I am as typical an Aranman as any scientist in search of evidence to bolster or demolish a theory could wish to find. The battery of scientists who have visited the islands over the years, measuring heads, taking samples of blood and impressions of teeth (not to mention the anthropologists who came to find out if the more bizarre sexual practices, described in the works of Mr Harold Robbins, existed in our community) have come to the conclusion that we are a very mixed lot from the racial viewpoint. This conclusion, which always seemed to shock everyone except the islanders, tended to be simplified by journalists to the more inaccurate statement that we were all descended from Cromwellian soldiers. This made a better headline.

As one who is more mixed than most, I find the whole business laughable in the extreme, as well as a great relief. What would we do if the scientists had found us so racially pure as to be inbred? That would make even better headlines.

My father came from Mount Scott, near Miltown Malbay in West Clare and would probably have taught school somewhere in that region had not a brother and cousin of his earned the undying enmity of the Bishop of Killaloe while fighting on the Republican side in the Civil

War. They ended up in jail and my father, who never fired a shot in anger in his life, was forced to seek employment where the Bishop's writ did not run.

He went to Inis Mór because he wished to master the Irish language, which was expiring rapidly in his own part of Clare, and because it was a convenient spot from which to keep an eye on the Bishop's health and the schools that became vacant in his diocese.

Many years later, when we were both cycling to Limerick to a match, I remember standing inside the door of Ennis Cathedral at mass, listening to Bishop Fogarty reading the gospel and the announcements in a strong, piercing voice and without benefit of amplification. When he eventually decided to join the Fenians in Heaven, Bishop Fogarty was nearly a hundred and I was older than my father had been when he arrived in Inis Mór.

My mother's people, on her father's side, were direct descendants of the Connemara O'Flahertys who were encouraged by Queen Elizabeth to direct their ferocity at the O'Brien clan that held sway in Aran, instead of attacking the City of the Tribes. Having thus rid herself of the O'Briens, the Queen handed the islands over to an adventurer from Athlone, one Sir John Rawson, and the O'Flahertys were left to scrape a living from the rocks and the turbulent sea.

But that strain was also mixed, as my grandfather had married the daughter of a man called Thomas Ganly who had come from Northern Protestant stock. An engineer by profession, he had supervised the building of Kilronan pier and Aerach Lighthouse. He married twice and fathered one spectacularly reckless son, Pat, who conducted a one-man campaign of terror against the local landlord's agent, his lackeys and livestock during the Land War.

I think all of this makes the point that the sea around the Aran Islands, far from being a barrier and a protector of racial and cultural purity, was conducive to change and brought us into contact with the mainland and the wide world beyond in many unexpected ways. For instance, it was the sea that introduced me to the world of soccer and cricket and the English public school at the age of nine when I had just seen my first inter-county game of Gaelic football.

In 1938 our lifeboat took part in two spectacular rescues and saved the crews of the English steam trawlers *Nogi* and *Hatano* from drowning, at great personal risk to the lifeboatmen. They were decorated for bravery in London and came home with medals and parchments and great stories that lost nothing in the telling.

Shortly afterwards, a new lifeboat, the *Frances, Mary and Edward* was based in Kilronan, complete with a radio officer called Roger Hammond, a brother of the famous England and Gloucestershire cricketer, Wally Hammond, one of the greatest batsmen the game has known.

The Hammonds had an only child, Roger, an overgrown but delicate boy of my own age. Because he was delicate and had endured long spells in hospital, Roger had a collection of toys, comics and sports annuals the like of which I had not even imagined. He had an anti-aircraft gun that fired and flamed, a set of electric trains that flew around an intricate maze of tracks, and an air-gun which was confined to barracks after Roger drew a target on an invitingly smooth and shiny surface and riddled the side of Pat Mullin's new currach. As well as all these toys, he had subscriptions to all the major boys' comics.

1939 was a fateful year for the world but for us in Aran it began with confirmation which, in those days, took place every fourth year. Poor Roger had no Irish and my father was too busy with his classes to be able to bring Roger's rudimentary knowledge of Christian doctrine up to the standard required by the Archdiocese of Tuam through the medium of the second official language of the state. Mrs Hammond, who was a convert, took this news very badly. It assumed the proportions of some sort of religious persecution.

My mother, who had no confirmation class and who was never happier than when performing the corporal works of mercy from mixed motives, took Roger in hand. She taught him patiently, found an understanding priest to examine him and he entered the ranks of good and perfect Christians like the rest of us to his mother's tearful joy. But I was to be the ultimate beneficiary.

As war became inevitable, Mr Hammond was summoned urgently to his military unit. The family furniture was sold locally and I was given all Roger's comics and annuais as a present. All through that winter and autumn, as Europe moved from phoney into real war, I sat under the oil lamp in our kitchen and entered the world of corner kicks, fagging, silly mid-off and Dave the Battling Dude.

As I was the eldest of a family of four and there was a four year gap between myself and my sister, Máirín, my parents had had plenty of time to teach me reading and writing, long before I went to school. Being a very committed member of Fianna Fáil, my father had the *Irish Press* on order in Powell's of Kilronan and I had all day to pore over the accumulated copies. The *Irish Independent*, the paper that had "called for the blood of James Connolly" a mere twenty years previously, never crossed our threshold, except when a page came wrapped around a loaf of bread.

Because there were no children to play with, I spent most of the day reading, or chatting to the succession of girls who minded me while my parents were in school and who were themselves waiting for the papers that would take them to America. Irish was the language of the house but as English was the dominant language in Kilronan, at that time, and as I spent part of every summer in Clare with my grandmother, I cannot remember a time when I did not read and speak both languages.

Soon I became a newspaper addict, reading every page carefully, even the incredibly tightly-packed full-page advertisements for Clery's sales. Then I became selective. Much to the dismay of my mother, who constantly scrutinised my character for signs of the less desirable traits of my ancestors on both sides, I began to collect murders as other children would collect stamps or cigarette cards.

Once when I was six she found me so engrossed in one of them that I did not hear her call me to my tea. It concerned an old farmer in Roscommon who died so suddenly and so painfully that his young wife was suspected of having hastened his end. Just as his coffin was being lowered into the grave, and feeling eyes full of suspicion boring holes through her, the young wife hurled herself on top of it shouting, "My darling, how will I live without you?" She was hauled out by the hair of her head by one of his brothers who made a caustic comment on her ability as an actress. The husband's body was subsequently exhumed and she was charged with poisoning him. Another, much younger, man was mentioned in the evidence . . .

After the lecture that followed, I promised to feed my imagination in future on the more wholesome pastures of Roddy the Rover, the sports pages and the contributions of Anna Kelly and M.J. McManus, but I did not have the slightest intention of avoiding the temptation of murder trials in future. I was just careful not to be seen and equally careful not to be drawn into conversation by trick comments such as, "That vagabond in Drumcondra deserves to be hanged".

At that time newspapers gave a lot of space to reporting murder trials and they were the subject of much discussion. Some of them were straightforward killings, connected with politics, land or revenge, but others gave an insight into the Hidden Ireland, into which reporters dared not venture without the imprimatur of the Central Criminal Court. This Hidden Ireland was not populated by wandering poets in the ancestral tongue but by philandering chemists with access to strychnine, randy mountainy farmers impregnating their wives' nubile nieces and silent young men from the Midlands who, after drinking twenty pints without uttering a single word, walked home through the stillness of the night and taking up an axe butchered the uncle whose land they hoped to inherit but whose filthy personal habits had driven them insane. I longed to get to know that world at first hand.

When we went to Galway we stayed in Mahon's Hotel in Foster Street, beside the big field where the circus pitched its tents when it came to town (now a public car park) and across the street from Rabbitt's Bar. Behind it was the railway station where the trains puffed and shunted all night. Down the street was Fahy's fascinating coach-building yard and around the corner, on Eyre Square, which was still surrounded by beautiful dark iron railings, a saddler's owned by the Grealish family. From memory I could draw a map of the streets of Galway from the door of Mahon's Hotel, through the Square, Williamsgate Street, Shop Street, Mainguard Street and Dominic Street as far as the Small Crane.

James Mahon was an Irish speaker, a Republican and a GAA man and he spoiled me in little ways that endeared him to me forever. On Saturdays, he allowed me to sit on a high stool in the public bar and talk to the tall men who wore long báinín jackets and black hats and spoke a type of Irish that was strange to my ears, being neither Aran nor Connemara. They were the second or third-last generation of native speakers from Tawin, Maree, Oranmore and Carnmore and among a lot of other things, I learned that what I called "iománaíocht" they called "báire" — as Raftery did and as the Connollys of Castlegar still do. They talked a lot about "báire".

Once we arrived in Galway on the *Dún Aengus* late on a Sunday night and I rose bright and early to watch James Mahon prepare the bar for business and smell the strange smells of the city. With the child's unerring instinct for the forbidden mysteries of the adult world, I realised that something strange was happening in the street and dodging past his restraining hand I ran out to see something being washed off the pavement and groups of people whispering about what had happened earlier that morning.

I was quickly whisked inside again and sent to breakfast, but I had heard enough to know that a man had been fatally injured by a blow of a hurley, after what was supposed to have been a victory celebration. The event had little to do with hurling but later, when I heard that the guilty party was a half twin and married and that his unmarried half twin had returned from England to swop places with his brother and serve the sentence for manslaughter, my interest in this new area of the Hidden Ireland was really awakened. That the story was probably made up after the event, was imperfectly heard and inaccurately retailed by some islander returned from the May Fair in Galway, mattered not at all. A child's imagination should never be constrained by too many facts but allowed to find its own boundaries.

At this stage of my development I associated the GAA almost completely with history. This was because my father had been in Croke Park on Bloody Sunday. He was a student in St Patrick's Training College, in Drumcondra, and had gone with some fellow-students to see the football match between Dublin and Tipperary.

His description of the panic when the shooting started, the stampede that flattened a galvanised fence, leaving him with a scar on his kneecap, was permanently locked in my memory by his fleeting image of a hawker whose basket of fruit was knocked over in the rush, down on her knees among the fleeing feet, trying to gather what she could and shrieking, "Jasus, me fine oranges!"

Now I discovered that my grandfather had played football for one of the first teams to be founded in Clare in the early years of the GAA, the Lord Clares. It was based in Miltown Malbay, and the surrounding area, and after Limerick Commercials won the first official All-Ireland final the Lord Clares played them in a challenge match in Ennis. The game ended in a certain amount of chaos but the Lord Clares claimed to have won. The goalkeeper was Johnny Marrinan, a next-door neighbour of my grandfather's who lived long enough for me to remember him clearly, and he told the story of how a female supporter of the Commercials tried to get the ball past him by whacking him on the head with a cabbage stump just as the ball landed in the goalmouth.

"Did you let it in?" the children would ask.

"Faith and I did not let it in! I held it!" he would answer, reliving his moment of triumph.

When the game came to an end he had to flee, carrying his good clothes, and the only safe place he could find to change was inside the railings of the O'Connell Monument in the centre of Ennis.

Although I barely remember my grandfather my hazy recollections are of a stocky man. In his playing days he weighed about sixteen stone and wore a broad leather belt around his waist. This, as well as the fact that he was well able to look after himself, makes all the more remarkable the feat performed by a man called Green from Cooraclare. While playing against the local team, near the Cross of Annagh, Green caught my grandfather by the leather belt and hurled him into a nearby stream.

The prospect of war now became a permanent topic of conversation and the radio began to dominate our kitchen. In Aran the constant fear was of American involvement; our own neutrality seemed to be taken for granted. In August 1939 I went with my parents to Dublin and I remember looking down into the streets behind Vaughan's Hotel on Parnell Square envying the children who played their games in such seemingly exotic surroundings. Apart from that I was impressed by the hiss and clatter of the trams, the smell of Woolworths, the song that was to be heard everywhere, "Roll out the Barrel", and my first visit to Croke Park.

Mayo and Kerry were playing in the All-Ireland football semi-final and my father took me on to the Cusack Stand. It was new and gleaming and huge and made a bigger impression on me than anything else, apart from the pitch itself which looked so smooth and out of place amid all the surrounding concrete.

Of the game I remember little, except that I cheered for the neighbours, Mayo, and was not too disappointed when the match ended in a draw. Paddy Moclair was playing for Mayo and he was well-known in Miltown Malbay where he had worked in a bank. It was said that when it became known in the area that a real, live bank clerk was playing gaelic football with Miltown, people travelled long distances to view this unusual happening.

What I remember of his play that day is hazy, apart from the fact that he seemed well able to deal with the robust Kerry backs, being as big and as bulky as any of them. Not so lucky, it seemed to me, was a small and very skilful corner forward called Tommy Hoban. More than once I was angered to see him hauled down by the jersey as he juggled with the ball. Many years later I met him in Westport and saw that while he was small in stature he was as solid as the back of the Reek.

My only other clear memory of the game concerned the goalkeeper, Tom Burke. Pádraig Puirséal picked him as the outstanding keeper of his own lifetime but I remember him for another reason: at the beginning of each half he bent down, scraped the soil with his fingers and crossed himself.

The excitement of being in this noisy place for the first time, as well as my anxiety to see Mayo win, seems to have blotted the Kerry team out of my memory completely, apart from the full-back line of Bill Myers, Joe Keohane and Tadhg Healy. I have a much clearer picture of the second game that was played that day, and a very historic game it was, for it was the only Ulster football final ever played in Croke Park. Cavan were playing Armagh and there in front of my eyes was Big Tom O'Reilly himself.

In the backs for Armagh was a very big man with a bandaged knee and among the forwards a very fast, fair-haired player who was clearly a star. The big man was Jim McCullough, playing with a bad injury; the fair-haired forward was Alf Murray, later President of the GAA.

Armagh were beaten and when I later asked why the game was played in Croke Park, I was told, vaguely, that there had been some sort of a row. And indeed there had, but not for years did I get to the bottom of it.

With the exception of 1938, when Monaghan beat them, Cavan were Ulster Champions from 1931 until 1945. When they played Armagh in Castleblaney in the 1939 final the walls around the pitch were flattened and when an Armagh player was jostled as he took a sideline throw, the crowd invaded the pitch and the match was abandoned. It was then decided to play it in Croke Park, there being no neutral venue in Ulster big enough to accommodate the expected crowd.

There was also bad blood between the counties; some say an element of it still lingers on to this day. It arose out of the rarest of happenings, a fatal accident during a game. Those who read Patrick Kavanagh's essay, "Gut Yer Man", or listen to Niall Tóibín deliver it, will find the incident mentioned there. Kavanagh relates a conversation between a worried mother and her son who is about to go off to play against Donaghmoyne. The mother expresses her fears:

"Many's the good man the same football put an end to. How I remember the poor Poochy Maguire that got the boot in the bottom of the belly and never overed it. If you take a fool's advice that you never took you'd lave the football alone."

"Things have changed since them days."

"That'll do you now. What about young Kiernan of Cross that was killed in Cavan?"

The strange thing is that the player who received the fatal injury was not called Kiernan at all. Whether for reasons of alliteration or regional reticence Kavanagh changed the name to another typical Crossmaglen surname. We shall respect his reasons, whatever they were, and leave it at that.

The All-Ireland hurling final of that year between Kilkenny and Cork will always be remembered as the "thunder and lightning" final. The stormy elements were a fitting backdrop to that morning's declaration of war. We were moving into a new house and my Aunt Annie was looking after the younger children. It was doubly difficult to follow the game, for as well as the bangs and crashes from the radio that punctuated Michael O'Hehir's commentary the kitchen was full of women on their way home from Mass, who had come for confirmation of the news of war. They moaned and prayed and sobbed and regarded it all as a sign from above. I remember nothing of the game, except that Kilkenny won by a point, but I can still hear the women and smell their sodden shawls.

A friend of mine who was in Croke Park had one vivid memory of the dreadful weather and the exciting match. A large priest from Kilkenny who sat behind him and at first encouraged the players to greater efforts with roars of "Kill him, you clown" and "Pull across the bastard", was obviously terrified of the storm and changed his tune dramatically to ejaculations of "Jesus, Mary and Joseph protect me" when a flash of lightning and a peal of thunder interrupted his bloodcurdling war cries.

2

But even the advent of World War Two was overshadowed
by a more immediate tragedy. Some months previously,
three men from Eoghnacht, near the western tip of Inis
Mór, were lost at sea as they returned from Connemara
in a currach, after a pilgrimage to Croagh Patrick. Seosamh
O Flannagáin was a native of Doolin, in Clare, and taught
with his wife in Eoghnacht school. Séamus O Flatharta
(Jamsie) was a man of exceptionally sharp wit and strik-
ing appearance and Seán O Direáin (Seáinín Tom) was a
seanchaí who had recorded stories for His Master's Voice
and appeared in a film directed by Robert Flaherty for the
Irish Folklore Commission. It was a stunning blow to the
community.

They were caught in a sudden squall, it seems. Two days
later a capsized currach was seen floating near Sand Head
in Inis Meáin. Our lifeboat went over to tow it home and
a big crowd gathered on the pier head in Kilronan. I remember the deathly silence and how all uncertainty and
hope were removed by three words from a young man
from Eoghnacht who was familiar with the currach in
which the men had travelled.

As the lifeboat came abreast of the pier head he removed
his cap and said, "'Sí atá ann". Their bodies were never
recovered.

My favourite aunt, Annie, was also stricken by a fatal
illness. She had worked in a variety of interesting jobs in
the United States and like her brother, Tom O'Flaherty,

had been involved in the struggles of organised labour there. A great mimic, she could sing all the Wobblie songs and she used to teach me various slang expressions that were in vogue in American eating-places in the 1920s, such as "Adam and Eve on a raft" (two fried eggs on toast) which was ordered with the instruction "Shipwreck 'em" if the eggs were to be done on both sides.

My mother's other brother, Liam, came and went suddenly and unexpectedly, as was his custom, but in an ever-deepening state of depression. He told us it was going to be a long war and then took off for the United States, not to be seen again by us until 1946. Occasionally we got newspaper cuttings of speeches he made in defence of Irish neutrality but after America entered the war even that contact was broken.

Once the German armies broke through the Maginot Line the war seemed to come closer and the radio took on an added importance in our lives. Our new house was built on very high ground, a mile west of Kilronan, and reception was excellent. A new curate, who understood electricity, operated a small windcharger and re-charged the low tension batteries, eliminating the necessity of sending them to Galway to be re-charged. This was just as well, for coal supplies for the *Dún Aengus* declined rapidly. The operating company, the Galway Bay Steamboat Company, added to their own difficulties and ours by selling some of their stocks to the Japanese liner that came to collect their nationals from Britain and Ireland. It struck us in Aran as charity beginning as far away from home as possible.

The *Dún Aengus* sailed twice weekly, and with some regularity, during the summer and early autumn, but in winter and early spring she sailed when the weather allowed her to service the three islands. Because of the excellent harbour at Kilronan we were not cut off as frequently as the other two islands, particularly Inis Meáin which has neither harbour nor shelter, but I do remember collecting ten copies of the *Irish Press* from Powell's one

Saturday morning in November and having a week-end orgy.

But for the news that kept the little flags moving on the *Daily Mail* war map of Europe that hung on our kitchen wall, we depended entirely on the radio. Fallon's of Galway, the electrical supplier with whom my father dealt, operated a quota system to give all customers a fair supply of the scarce high tension batteries. This quota was not equal to our demands. As well as the news, the games, Seán O Ceallacháin's Gaelic Sports Results and Question Time, there were schools programmes, the Sunday night play, céilí music – in fact, we listened to almost everything Radio Eireann transmitted – and there was Lord Haw Haw.

William Joyce was listened to regularly in the West, wherever radios functioned. I remember one very wild and wet night in October, doing my lessons in the kitchen with my father and wondering who had come knocking at our door so late on such a night. A Connemara boatman stood on the threshold and before my father had time to say that we had already bought turf for both household and school, the man asked him if our radio was working as he had been led to believe in a pub in Kilronan.

"Ba mhaith liom éisteacht leis an Seoigeach seo ar a dtugann siad Lord Haw Haw" (I would like to hear this Joyce they call Lord Haw Haw), he said.

We sat at the range and drank tea and his clothes gave off clouds of steam as we listened to the strange strangulated accent coming loud and clear from Berlin. When he finished, the radio was switched off; the boatman got up to go, thanked us and said, "Bhuel, is diabhlaí breá an cainteoir é" (Well, he's a bloody fine talker) and went back to his boat.

Whenever I think of radio programmes during those war years, I remember Brian Fitzpatrick with special affection. Brian was from Kileaney and through his good offices we had an adequate radio service instead of a curtailed one. The English steam trawlers fished off the islands all through the war and put into Kilronan, to supplement their supplies, whenever they could. Brian had a good relationship with a number of skippers and, as a result, we got additional high tension batteries.

Years later, when I was working in England, I met an ex-serviceman on a train between King's Cross and Grimsby who took me severely to task for coming from a place where the crews of German U-Boats were given food, drink and hospitality in England's hour of need. I did not have the heart to tell him that the irony of reality was that the news that moved my little swastikas forward on the map and my little Union Jacks backwards, in those early years of the war, came courtesy of a system of barter that also lubricated the morale of Swansea fishermen.

In the autumn of 1940 life was still reasonably normal. My father took me to Dublin for a long weekend and I saw my first All-Ireland hurling final. While shopping in Elvery's he was offered two Cusack Stand tickets for the match between Limerick and Kilkenny. It seemed too good to be true and I spent the night sleeping fitfully, worried that my father would lose the tickets and that the two of us would be left standing outside Croke Park, listening to the roars of the crowd and pleading in vain with stony-faced officials.

But everything went smoothly and unlike my previous visit, when I found the surroundings more interesting than the performance, I was clearly aware that I was in the presence of some of the greatest hurlers of all time. I was by now reading the sports pages almost as eagerly as I read the murder trials. On to the field came the Mackeys, Mick and John, Dick Stokes, Paddy Scanlon (the great goalkeeper who worked in McDonough's of Galway), Paddy Clohessy, Jim Langton, Paddy Grace, Jimmy O'Connell, Jackie Power, Jack Mulcahy and the others who had previously been only names on Michael O'Hehir's lips or smudgy photographs in the newspaper.

I got into the swing of Croke Park in no time at all and even took issue with a large priest from Kilkenny who was sitting behind me. He took grave exception to a stroke which felled Jack Gargan and began to roar, "The line! The line!" at the referee and Paddy Clohessy simultaneously. In a manner far too advanced for my years, and for his level of tolerance, I told him it was an accident and voiced concern for his eyesight. I got a dig of an umbrella from the priest and was advised by my father to keep my eyes on the field and my mouth shut.

But I had the last laugh. My favourites, Limerick, won by two clear goals. Little did anyone present imagine that internal dissension and strife would soon relegate Limerick hurlers to the lower depths inhabited by both Clare and Galway for so many years. Limerick won a National League final in 1946 but did not win another Munster senior championship until 1955 and had to wait until 1973 to win another All-Ireland.

After that it was back to Aran, the war and the radio. The war had now come to our very shores as the sea washed up bodies of drowned sailors and airmen, German, British and, later, American. They were buried in two of the island's cemeteries and later exhumed for burial at home, or in the German cemetery at Glencree, with the exception of a young Scottish airman. He had baled out of his blazing aircraft early one morning, over the bay, and was hauled up in a net later that day, strangled by his parachute. He was buried in the graveyard at Cnocán na mBan, overlooking the beautiful beach at Kilmurvey, and when his parents came to see his grave, after the war, they liked the place so much and were so appreciative of the way the grave had been tended, that they decided to leave his remains in Aran soil forever.

Then there was the flotsam: bales of rubber and cotton, spars and planks, abandoned lifeboats and life-rafts, lumps of tallow which were melted down and made into candles and even a cask of rum that got a sudden and happy death.

One Sunday morning a mine was seen lodged behind some boulders at the foot of a cliff. It was a harmless looking rusty object and not at all sinister. A crowd gathered on the cliff-top and some of the more foolhardy began to use it as a cockshot until the gardaí arrived and cleared the area. Later, when the army explosive experts arrived from Athlone and detonated it, part of the cliff-face and the boulders that had trapped it were blown to smithereens. Strange metal objects from the sea were subsequently given a very wide berth.

One would have imagined that the recent tragedy months before in Annagaire, in the Donegal Gaeltacht, where several young people were blown to pieces by a mine which they were trying to prise open, would have been sufficient warning to everyone along the coast. Some years later, when I was in boarding school, the boys from Gaoth Dobhair and the Rosses had strange stories to tell in the dormitories at night, of how the White Lady who was reputed to have appeared on a rock-face at nearby Kerry-town about that time, had tried to warn the people of the impending disaster by pointing her finger in the direction of the foreshore where the mine was washed up.

There were also comic interludes. A little Englishman, whose surname was Marcus, and who, like Mrs Hammond, was another convert to Catholicism, had settled among us and began to show an unhealthy interest in matters that should have been none of his business, according to the local gardaí. They searched his hotel room and found copious notes on the Coast Watching service, the gardaí and the political views of all public servants on the island. I remember that my father and Dr Jim O'Brien, our doctor, were described as likely to aid the German forces if they invaded us. Poor Mr Marcus, who was in reality a draft dodger playing at being a spy, was banished forthwith to inland parts and we never heard of him again.

Dr O'Brien, who had a lot of money and property and who was in fact very pro-British but had been trying to find out if the little convert had any patriotic streak in him, was very annoyed by the affair. He was even more annoyed to find out that Mr Marcus had departed with one of his precious books: a crime infinitely worse than spying.

Dr Heinrich Becker, a German folklorist who spent the war years in Ireland, some of them in Inis Mór, was also mentioned in dispatches by our amateur spy. I must confess that I was a bit suspicious of him myself ever since the day he so ostentatiously disregarded news of the German invasion of Norway while discussing some folkloric subject with my father, who was straining his other ear to the radio news.

Dr Becker was a talented musician as well as being a folklorist and was even able to play tunes on a saw. This he did to amuse his landlord who boasted in the pub that his German lodger could make a fortune if he chose to go on the stage. But the local practical jokers, who did so much to enliven island life, decided to have some fun and they told the landlord that he would be well advised to keep an eye on his guest.

They found it significant that his playing always took place at night, when the German U-Boats, to which Dr Becker was undoubtedly transmitting military secrets with his saw, were able to come into the shelter of the cliffs and surface under cover of darkness. The joke almost got out of control when it was pointed out to the landlord that men were locked up in the Curragh without trial for far less than being involved with a spy.

Dr Becker spent many years visiting the Aran Islands after the war but I never did find out if he was aware of the folklore he had almost created. I almost told the story to my man on the train between King's Cross and Grimsby but thought better of it. Folklore of that kind was appearing as news in some of the more prominent English newspapers at the time.

In Clare the war seemed more remote while its effects were far more keenly felt than they were in Aran. My grandmother and all her neighbours never ceased to moan about the scarcity of tea and sugar, but particularly tea, which was fetching a pound a pound on the black market: five or six times its controlled price. Unlike Aran, where there were no bogs and we did not have to worry too much about hay, as the livestock could be left to graze in the fields all year round, gallons of tea were required in Clare during the hay-making and turf-harvesting seasons. Indeed, I shall always savour the memory of tea drunk from a bottle while eating fresh griddle-cake in a meadow or on the bog on the slopes of Mount Callan. I was having the best of all worlds in those years.

I noticed that my father was regarded in Clare as an expert on the conduct of the war; perhaps because he seemed to those who lived on the mainland to view the fighting from an eminence in the Atlantic, closer to the battle of the North Atlantic. Certainly, nobody in west Clare seemed very interested in Lord Haw Haw and even less in the other gentleman who sometimes addressed us from Germany in the sweet and kingly tongue of the Gael.

One Sunday after mass, in a pub in Miltown Malbay, my father and two other teachers were locked in a discussion about Hitler's intentions in North Africa. My uncle, Tomás, was sitting on a stool, bored stiff. When the discussion was about to peter out, one of the school teachers was struck by another thought.

"But what will he do when his army reaches Cairo?" he asked.

"Bedamned to him," said Tomás, suddenly. "What we want to know is what will happen when Kilmurray meet Cooraclare at three o'clock today!"

It was in the company of my Uncle Tomás, who inherited the family farm, that I came to know various facets of life, including the GAA, at the most interesting human level. Football in west Clare was full of history and as with everything else in that most remarkable of Irish counties, countless hours were spent "tracing" every detail of the politics, family history and social background of all participants. It was bubbling with life and fun and even scandal.

Once Tomás took me on the crossbar of his bike to a match at which a row started between two bands as to which of them would have place of honour in the pre-match parade — or something of that nature. It really was not about that at all. One band seemed to have stronger political views than the other, for its members and supporters referred loudly to the others as "Free Staters", "Blueshirts" and other low forms of Irish political life. At one stage the big drum was seized by a man who threatened to put it out of action with his boot.

This was great stuff, but when I tried to wriggle closer to the action I was hauled back by the scruff of the neck by Tomás.

"If you are trampled to death," he wanted to know, "how the hell am I going to explain it to your father and mother?"

Then a priest arrived and called everyone to order. He was very angry and said that the affair was an affront to his own authority, as a priest and an officer of the GAA. But he was clearly not neutral, for he addressed the leader of the republican band as a "blackguard" who had come to make mischief.

As if we didn't have it in our own house, I thought to myself, the church triumphant rules here also. But no sooner had that thought lodged itself in my mind than up spoke a little piper in a green kilt who addressed the priest loudly, informing him that it was hard for them to take him seriously in either one of his two offices. Now, if he stopped drinking whiskey after hours, in a certain named public house, in the company of various named citizens – male and female – then he, the piper, might even listen to him with a little respect.

When somebody in the background suggested that a blue shirt would look better on the priest than the black one he was wearing, my Uncle Tomás hauled me off out of earshot and refused point-blank to discuss the matter with me later as we headed for home after the match. But that night, when I was supposed to be asleep in bed, I crept down and listened at the kitchen door as Tomás gave my grandmother a richly-embellished version of the day's happenings with many illuminating footnotes.

Just after the outbreak of war one of the county footballers came to work in Inis Mór. He was Pat Mór Mac Donncha from Ros a' Mhíl who came to replace Seosamh O Flannagáin in Eoghnacht school until the eldest of O Flannagáin's family had come through the training college. Big Pat was really big. He played at full forward in the 1941 All-Ireland against Kerry and although I had not yet made the acquaintance of the Kerry full back, Joe Keohane, whenever I saw Big Pat cycle past our house on his racer, which looked like a child's bicycle beneath his great bulk, I imagined Joe Keohane as some sort of giant.

Also on that team in 1941 was another Pat McDonough, christened Small Pat to distinguish him from his Ros a' Mhíl namesake. Small Pat, who was from Tuam and played in the backs, was not small at all and he was also part of a Galway team that had many stars and very few All-Irelands to show for their considerable efforts.

The Kerry footballers were the bane of my youthful life. Apart from Joe Keohane, who now inhabited a special corner of my imagination, the rest of them seemed to inhabit the same world as the Cannonball Kid, or indeed, Fianna Eireann. Only when I saw some of them at close quarters, at half-time in a National League match against Galway in the Sportsground, taking swigs out of a brandy bottle to fortify them against the bitter March wind, did they assume human proportions.

Between 1929 and 1932, Kerry won four All-Irelands in a row. Then Cavan, Galway, Cavan and Mayo bridged the years until 1937 when Kerry won again. The way I heard it told in Kerry, many years later, the team was set for another long run until Galway beat them in a replay in 1938 — an indignity which the county had not previously suffered. With hindsight, Galway came between Kerry and those elusive five titles in a row for Kerry won again in 1939, 1940 and 1941, beating us on two occasions and Meath on the other.

All that was bad enough if worse were not to follow. In 1942, Bobbie Beggs from Skerries, who had come to Galway to work and soon became one of Galway's football giants at centre half back, returned to his native county. To this day he is held in affection and high esteem by generations of Galwegians who never saw him play. Even the events of 1942 are long forgiven him. For Bobbie Beggs declared for Dublin and faced Galway in the final.

Having beaten Kerry by a single goal in the semi-final, Galway looked set for success. Seán Thornton from Spiddal was the top scorer all through the championship. Bobbie Beggs, who was marking him was, according to popular superstition, way past his best.

This is the first final that I can recall almost entirely from Michael O'Hehir's commentary. It was a good one but Bobbie Beggs played a blinder and we lost by two points. Big Pat McDonough did not play that day. Working in Aran and trying to train and get to the mainland for matches was well nigh impossible, even in normal times.

Another member of the Galway team of that period also spent some time in Inis Mór. Joe Duggan was an engineer with Galway County Council and was a champion discus thrower as well as a footballer. His prowess with weights was of more importance in Inis Mór than his footballing skills but I remember him as one of the two finest-looking mainlanders I saw during those years, the other being Séamus Ennis.

Neither Big Pat McDonough nor Joe Duggan managed to win All-Ireland medals but Joe's son, Jimmy, was on the team that won the third All-Ireland in a row for Galway in 1966, at eighteen years of age. Big Pat's nephew, Cóilín, was also a member of that team.

Now, at the age of thirteen, the mainland was coming closer. It was decided that I would go to secondary school and that meant some boarding school on the mainland. My father organised scholarship classes for County Council, Gaeltacht and Preparatory Colleges examinations. In 1943 I had the distinction of failing, not alone the handwriting test and arithmetic in the Preparatory Colleges examination, but also Irish.

Had I sat up for a week plotting ways of humiliating my parents I could scarcely have bettered my unplanned disgrace. To make matters much worse for me, Pádraig O Goill who was a whole year younger than I was, won a scholarship to St Mary's in Galway. I was only too keenly aware of the glee with which all right-thinking rascals would regard the exposure of the teachers' eldest son as a certified dunce. All too easily I could imagine myself in any of their shoes.

All that autumn, through the winter and into the spring of 1944, there was little time for reading comics, murder trials, or even the sports pages (although I was aware that a new star had risen in the east and stood over the village of Knockcroghery, in Roscommon) as I was out through hoops, at school and again at home, in an effort to concentrate my mind on the hard facts of life.

Although I tried to hide it under a bushel of bravado, I was ashamed of my bad performance and determined to do better at the second attempt. The foundations of any aptitude I have developed in writing Irish dates from that struggle with the Preparatory Colleges examination. This time I passed and was called to Coláiste Einde in Salthill, but because the building had been taken over as a military hospital, I was told to stand by for further instructions. So an element of mystery was added to the prospect of impending adventures on the mainland of Ireland.

Now that the Preparatory Colleges are a thing of the past, I should explain that the system was established as a means of recruiting students who would be fluent in Irish before they entered the Training Colleges. Entrance was by nationwide public examination, held at Easter, and half the places were reserved for successful candidates from the Gaeltacht.

There were two colleges for boys: Coláiste Iosagáin, Baile Mhúirne and Coláiste Einde in Salthill. There were four colleges for girls: Coláiste Íde in Corca Dhuibhne, Coláiste Mhuire, Tuar Mhic Eada, Coláiste Bhríde, Fál Carrach and Coláiste Moibhí in Shanganagh Castle, near

Bray, which catered for Protestant girls. All the colleges were residential, the Inter and Leaving Certificate courses were completed in four years and successful students were assured of places in the Training Colleges. I shall deal briefly with the system, and the events leading to its abolition, later.

3

Brendan Behan had a story about being in Paris one summer and going for a walk with Samuel Beckett. The incident occurred during the fifties when Brendan wrote a weekly column for the *Irish Press* which was accompanied by a photograph of his very recognisable head. As the two walked along, Brendan was spotted by three young Irish clerics on their way home from Rome after ordination. They addressed him in Irish and as they were going in the same direction joined himself and Beckett in their walk.

Two of them walked on either side of Brendan and as there was no more room on the pavement the third man walked behind them with a silent Beckett. The young priest was full of talk and wanted to know when Beckett had last visited home. Beckett replied that he had not been home for years. His companion thought that was a shame and wanted to know if he intended to return in the near future.

"I have been invited to Dublin in September," said Beckett, with little enthusiasm.

"What time in September, Mr Beckett?"

"Sometime in the middle of the month, I think."

"Yerra sure, what harm," said the young priest kindly, "You'll miss the hurling but you'll be there for the football."

The story reminded me of my departure to Coláiste Einde in the autumn of 1944. We had heard that we were to be lodged in St Patrick's Training College, in

Drumcondra, which was vacant because teachers were not being trained for some years in the forties. My first thought was that, with a bit of luck, I would see the two All-Irelands. But the telegram arrived just before the football final and a sudden break in the weather had prevented the *Dún Aengus* from sailing. So I sat for four days with my bag packed, gazing down along the bay and praying for fine weather.

On the evening of the fifth day, my father rushed home early from school telling me to grab my bag and head for the pier as the O'Brien brothers from Sruthán were unloading turf and would sail within the hour. There was no time for tearful farewells and we were soon heading for Casla bay in a brisk south-easterly breeze and choppy sea. My father went into the little fo'c'sle under the forepeak, where there was shelter, and warmth but I was far too excited to miss any part of the adventure. I huddled close to the helmsman, fantasising and getting soaked to the skin.

The following morning we got the bus to Galway and another bus to Dublin which seemed to call at every town in the Midlands before dropping us on the quays in the afternoon. Classes were still in progress and an tAthair Pádraig O Laoi, who showed me my cubicle in the huge dormitory, told me to report back at bed-time. My father, who had not visited the college since 1922, was anxious to explore the place but I hauled him across the road to the pictures in the Drumcondra Grand cinema.

I would probably have long forgotten the details of that first day, for I was exhausted, over-excited and developing a heavy cold as a result of my wetting in Galway bay, but the picture we saw was an exceptionally good war film, based on a true tale of a ship adrift at sea, called *San Demetrio, London* in which I heard Irish spoken on the screen for the first time.

The following morning I woke with a high temperature and running nose and the school matron was called to examine me. But I was not alone in the dormitory, however, as a classmate from Gaoth Dobhair, Seán O Gallchóir, had decided to test the system's defences against maling-erers. He was sleeping two cubicles away from me but he was playing his part seriously and refused to speak a word until the matron arrived.

She saw what my problem was, prescribed aspirin and hot drinks and told me to stay in bed for a few days. She then went to Seán's cubicle and asked him what the matter was. He let fly a machine-gunned sentence of Donegal Irish while rattling a lot of saliva in his gullet. Not one word could she understand. Question and answer were repeated twice but to no avail. She returned to my cubicle and asked me to construe. When I told her that the illnesses men-tioned were new to me also she wanted to know if I was a genuine native speaker at all and not just a learner like herself. I was beginning to enjoy myself, for the matron was good-looking and smelt very sweetly as well.

I suggested that Seán might explain his strange ailments to both of us in the second official language of the state. In Coláiste Einde it was spoken only during English class and trying to get a pupil to explain imaginary illnesses through its medium was a fairly delicate matter. But Seán, who was discovering all manners of loopholes in the system, did the helpful thing, displaying a command of English which, if it were genuine, would have failed him the entrance examination many times over.

Thus did I learn my first lesson in the Donegal dialect of Irish. For what Seán had been saying to us was, "Tá sceadamán nimhneach agam agus tá déideadh orm." And if I wanted to tell the matron that I had a sore throat and toothache, I would have said, "Tá scórnach tinn agam agus tá daitheacha fiacaile orm."

It was a good introduction to life in Coláiste Einde and gave me an insight into the problems that faced those stu-dents who came from parts of the country where Irish had not been spoken for decades.

During my four years in Coláiste Einde all the living dialects of Irish, with the exception of the Déise, were spoken there. There were also students from the non-

Gaeltacht areas of Donegal, Mayo and Galway as well as boys from Cavan, Leitrim, Monaghan, Louth, Meath, Westmeath, Clare and Tipperary. Linguistically it was like a vat into which almost all the dialects and regional accents were poured and out of which something close to a standard speech, based on the living language, emerged; complete with the school argot which perplexed our parents as well as the teams that played against us, even when they were from schools where subjects were taught through Irish. Only in the First Irish-speaking battalion, when it was in its heyday in Renmore, have I heard of this kind of development.

Because we were being prepared for a specific purpose the curriculum differed from that of the other secondary schools — as did the school's status, for we were administered directly by the Department of Education. Modern languages were not taught, but we learned Latin as well as Irish, English, History, Geography, Physics, Mathematics and Christian Doctrine. Music and Drawing were also compulsory as was Woodwork, up to Intermediate Certificate, and we had elocution classes in our final year.

Considering that all this was packed into four years and that failure in either one of the certificate examinations meant the end of this particular academic road, it is hardly surprising that the emphasis was on studying and passing the examinations and that everything else, including sport, was of secondary importance.

But, in theory at least, games were also compulsory and football boots and togs were included in the list of essential kit. But in time, those who wanted to play football and those who were not interested in team sports were allowed to go their respective ways, except on rare occasions — usually a bitter cold day in spring — when one of the priests would be moved by an attack of sadism and order all hands on to the football field.

Then, to the glee of the more robust hooligans, the non-footballers would appear in a white-skinned and shivering line. When they were assigned to a team they were careful to keep well out on the sideline, trotting up and down and blowing on their hands, avoiding play except when they were enveloped in a planned mêlée and subjected to good-natured but most unwelcome horsing.

My class of eighteen was composed of ten from Donegal (backboned by five lively spirits from Gaoth Dobhair), four from Mayo, three from Galway, and Seán Mac Iomhair kept a lone flag flying for Dundalk. We seemed to get on very well together from the beginning and I do not remember any tension in the group; apart from one memorable occasion when one of our number fleeced all the other gamblers at pontoon, using a carefully doctored deck of cards, and bought a pair of flashy shoes with the proceeds. Even at this stage in the narrative readers might be tempted to guess his identity.

That first year in Dublin flew past at great speed. All our free time was packed with activity. Rationing was at its peak and although the end of the war in Europe was in sight, food and fuel were in short supply, and there were constant arguments in the refectory about cutting the loaves of bread and dividing the potatoes and the tiny balls of butter.

We also had a deal of freedom which we almost took for granted. On Sundays we were marched off to Croke Park if there was any match of interest being played; all matches were of interest to us, of course. But when there were no matches we were taken to other places of interest in the city, to the cinema occasionally, to Oireachtas na Gaeilge and to an art exhibition, on one unforgettable day, when we passed by Trinity College on the tram, gazing silently at its battle-scarred facade with not a pane of glass intact. Our teachers had told us of the attack by an infuriated crowd who did not appreciate the burning of the Tricolour and the raising of the Union Jack in its stead on the flag-staff, by students who had been using the college as a funk-hole during the war which had just ended.

The end of the war I remember vividly. I had just come out of class and was running out to the football pitch when

I ran into Pádraig O Conaola from Ros a' Mhíl (the college janitor who had accompanied it from Galway) who held up a copy of the *Evening Herald* with a huge headline announcing Hitler's suicide. We had just come through the coldest winter I ever endured and for the first time in my life I had actually held snow in my hands. My interest in the snow caused huge merriment among my classmates who did not realise that it rarely ever lodged in Aran, the flakes dissolving as they approached the ground.

Travelling home for Christmas was a great adventure, as I was booking into hotels on my own for the first time. In Galway I stayed in the American Hotel on Eyre Square, which was where my family stayed after Mahon's had gone out of business. That first Christmas I shared a room with a Christian Brother and a lighthouse keeper from Kerry who was stationed on Aerach Rock. He was a Protestant and was contemplating marriage with a young Catholic lady in Galway. The usual impediments had taken on sufficient importance in their lives to have caused a disagreement and he had taken to the drink. He had been joined by the Christian Brother.

They passed the lighthouse keeper's bottle of whiskey from bed to bed and talked religion. I could not sleep and hated them both, for I was sure I would over-sleep, not be called in time, miss the *Dún Aengus* and spend Christmas miserably in a hotel in Galway. Just as they seemed to be dozing off the lighthouse keeper rose up on his elbow in the bed and said:

"And I wouldn't mind, Brother, but there is damn all difference between us in the end. I worship the Father and you worship the Mother and isn't it all the same family?"

This was too much for the Christian Brother who also rose up, called for the bottle and brought some theological sanity to the situation by saying:

"Do you realise, my poor *amadán*, that you're talking through your bloody arse?"

They both fell asleep eventually and snored like porpoises and I decided to stay awake for safety's sake, getting up every quarter of an hour and dousing my face with cold water, until it was an hour before sailing time when I headed for the docks. The *Dún Aengus* was there, lying low in the water, her portholes gleaming like golden discs, and the rasp of Mike Geary's shovel on the stokehold floor echoing around the silent docks as he hurled inferior coal under the boiler to raise enough steam to get us home.

Down in the cabin, the students from the three islands gathered and talked earnestly about school. Most of the talk concerned food, or the lack of it, and it seemed to me that in comparison with some of the other colleges we were living in luxury in Coláiste Einde. Tales of hunger pangs from St Jarlath's College were particularly memorable.

On my way back to Dublin, after Christmas, I had my teeth seen to in Galway and barely caught the mail train. Somewhere between Moate and Mullingar it stopped without reason or warning, all the lights dimmed and we were left shivering in ignorance for over an hour while men carrying lanterns walked up and down beside the train shouting unintelligibly.

We finally arrived in Westland Row in the small hours and myself and a young man from Athlone, who was returning to England, booked into the only premises in the area that seemed prepared to admit us. It was a strange kind of seedy boarding house and in normal circumstances its squalor would have scared me out of a year's growth. Even at that hour of the morning, sounds of laughter, the clinking of glasses and female voices came from a room at the back. We were asked to pay in advance by an evil-looking hunchback who showed us to our room by the light of a flashlamp.

We were sharing a bed, which was just as well, for the room was even colder than the train. Just as I was about to fall asleep, a man and a woman came lurching up the stairs, laughing loudly. They went into a nearby room and crashed on to a bed which shortly began to heave and creak like the *Dún Aengus* on a bad day in the Foul Sound.

The man from Athlone bounded out of bed, grabbed the

chair on which we had left our clothes and rammed it hard under the door-knob and against the floor, muttering, "Feckin' knockin' shop". He removed our wallets from under the pillow and placed them under the mattress, directly beneath our bodies. He then rummaged in his suitcase and took out something which he placed in his shoe, putting that under his side of the pillow. In the morning I discovered that the object was an old-fashioned cut-throat razor.

In the morning light, the place looked drab, dirty and depressing and I stole away, breakfastless, and caught an early tram to Drumcondra. When I reported myself to the president, to explain my late arrival, he wanted to know where I had spent the night. I told him that I had been very comfortable in the Grosvenor Hotel.

But things change slowly in Ireland, at certain levels, and on the night the *Evening Mail* appeared for the last time I went with some companions on a sentimental journey to the old kip. We had been at the deceased paper's wake and were in search of more drink and devilment. But we had to beat a hasty retreat when the boys in blue arrived, looking for a nimble-fingered lady who had relieved a cattle-dealer of his wallet in an establishment near the cattle market. We went over the back wall and sought sanctuary in a more respectable premises.

I played my first game of competitive football that year also, against a team from a boys' club in Whitehall. I was put in goal and by happy accident found myself in that reasonably soft berth for the next two years. It happened when one of our backs gave away a penalty and I was in a situation I had read about scores of times in boy's fiction. The player who came to take the kick was a beefy block of a fellow who, judging from the comments of his team-mates, had been putting away penalties since he learned to walk. I was hoping that he would put it past my reach so that I could dive spectacularly but instead he hit it straight at me and almost stuck my navel to my backbone. Reflex action and a sharp pain forced me to hold on to it and I was left with very sore stomach muscles and a reputation as a sound goalkeeper.

Our senior football team played lots of matches but they lost in the first round of the Leinster senior colleges championship against Dundalk CBS, a game which they were expected to win. In those days, as best I remember, boarding schools looked down on day schools when it came to football. That was certainly the case in Connacht.

But for those of us who were in first year, and not yet involved in inter-school matches, going to Croke Park to see the great teams and the great players was much more interesting than playing. We were returning to Galway the following year and knew that there were going to be few opportunities of seeing big matches there.

Roscommon were the stars of the All-Ireland final of 1944. Some of our seniors, who arrived in the college in time to see the All-Ireland final, had hair-raising stories to tell of the crush on the Canal End and of girls fainting in the front of the crowd and being passed out to the St John's Ambulance men, by hand, over the heads of those behind them. Despite the war and petrol rationing, almost 80,000 people saw Roscommon beat Kerry and win their second final in succession. Years later, when I was travelling around Ireland, I met people who had come to see that match by the most extraordinary means — including one party from north Kerry who hired a traveller's caravan in Limerick and travelled to the outskirts of Dublin, complete with driver.

The first time I saw Roscommon play was in the final of some tournament or other against Carlow. Carlow had won the Leinster Championship in 1944 and were only beaten by two points by Kerry in the All-Ireland semi-final. One of their mid-fielders, Jim Morris, practised in the playing field at St Patrick's College with some other county players, including Frankie Byrne of Meath, who taught in the national school attached to the College. But the players I remember best were Bill Carlos of Roscommon, a real giant of a man who drove a drop kick all of seventy yards into the Carlow goal and the Carlow right half back, Paddy Whelan, who was bald and was a half back in the style of Christo Hand, "Red" Collier and Gerry O'Reilly. It is worth mentioning that Bill Carlos, who emigrated to the United States and played in various Brendan Cup competitions with New York, won an All-Ireland medal for hurling with Connacht Colleges on the only occasion when they won that particular competition.

We also noticed that day something that Michael O'Hehir had often remarked on in his commentaries: that the scoreboard operator always bent down to pick up the next number after the one that indicated Roscommon's total of points whenever Donal Keenan came up to take a close free.

Mention of Carlow will probably surprise those who regard the county as one of the Cinderellas of football, which it has been for many years now. Whatever about the rise or decline in standards and the state of the rules of football, there seemed to be more equality of standard in Leinster and Connacht in those days than there is at present.

Between 1940 and 1950, Leinster senior titles were won by Meath, Dublin, Louth, Carlow, Wexford and Laois, while Westmeath and Kildare contested finals. In Connacht, during the same period, the titles were shared almost equally between Mayo, Galway and Roscommon. Only in the case of Ulster and Munster does my proposition fall on its face.

In Ulster, Cavan occupied the position that Kerry now commands in Munster but in the intervening years all counties, with the exception of Fermanagh, have won provincial titles. Munster offers the same choice then as now: Kerry and Cork in unequal proportions.

We saw many games between units of the Army. Some of the best hurlers and footballers in the country were members of the armed forces during the war that we called "The Emergency". To emphasise that point and direct the minds of young athletes towards the proper, patriotic path, county players were given their military ranks in match reports. This largely forgotten facet of contemporary history is preserved in a folkloric sentence uttered by Seán O Ceallacháin on radio, at this time: "The turning point of this match came mid-way through the second half when Sergeant Jack McQuillan rounded Lieutenant Joe Keohane and slammed a major to the net".

Army games, as I remember them, were always very clean and sporting but never very serious. Very different was a Fitzgibbon Cup game between UCD and UCC in the course of which most of the thirty players did battle for long periods, with officials and substitutes joining in. The clean Fitzgibbon hurler, in those days, was the one who dropped his hurley and hit you with his fist.

When the Railway Cup semi-final between Leinster and Ulster was played in Croke Park, in February 1945, the Donegal boys, who formed the biggest ethnic group in Coláiste Einde, had their great moment. Hudie Beag Gallagher from Bun Beag, one of the great corner forwards of his day and the best the county has produced, was lining out for Ulster. At night in the dormitory tales were told of his exploits: the Gaoth Dobhair contingent having particularly graphic accounts of battles against Dungloe played in far-off Letterkenny. The eyes of Coláiste Einde were on Hudie Beag.

Nor did the man from Bun Beag disappoint us. He scored a great goal in the first game, that ended in a draw. The dormitory that night was like the roosting-place of a thousand starlings.

Unfortunately, the might of Leinster prevailed on the second occasion and they went on to beat Connacht in the final. But Hudie Beag had already won two Railway Cup medals with Ulster and got an opportunity to pit his skills against the best backs in Ireland at the time. It also enabled those of us who had not yet crossed The Black Pig's Dyke to see him in action. That was one of the great attractions of the Railway Cup competition.

The finals on St Patrick's Day were memorable for the

appearance of a player whom I never expected to see in action, as he was then almost at the end of his distinguished career. But in the second half of the football final who should come on as a substitute but Tommy Murphy of Laois. I remember the roar of the crowd when he caught the first ball but I remember little else except that in a curious way I knew even then that I would boast that I had seen Tommy Murphy play football.

Much sharper are my recollections of one of the greatest forwards I have ever seen, a player who had little going for him as a gaelic footballer apart from his skill. Iggy Jones from Dungannon played with a great St Patrick's Armagh team that included the Devlin brothers, Jim and Eddie. They all played with Tyrone in the fifties but were playing with Ulster Colleges when I saw them.

Iggy Jones was about five foot six and was very slightly built, but his speed, ball control, side-step and particularly his ground shot for goal put him in a class apart. He was the best controller of the ball on a solo-run that I have seen and Pádraig Puirséal, who saw all the great players between 1930 and the mid-sixties, has paid his own considered tribute to him. Unfortunately, as we shall see later, the rules of gaelic football were unable to protect him from opponents who had no answer to his skills, except the use of brute force, when he began to play senior county football.

I regret not having seen the two Hogan Cup finals between St Patrick's, Armagh and St Jarlath's, Tuam: in 1946 when Armagh won (Iggy Jones scoring 3-4 of his team's 3-11) and in 1947 when Jarlath's had their revenge (Seán Purcell giving an exhibition of all-round excellence). I have merely met the scholars and they rate these two games as the best examples of highly competitive gaelic football, at that level.

A lot of the credit for the fast, open play that distinguished that particular competition at the time, and for years afterwards, must be given to those who prepared the teams and gave them their instructions. To them also must be given the credit for the absence of the ghastly "professional" foul that so disfigures even that competition today. If schools' players are not alone encouraged but instructed to win at all costs, there can be little room left for sportsmanship, except as an abstract subject in an essay.

But if Croke Park was the centre of our attention in the course of the year, our school's greatest triumph occurred on the track at Iveagh Grounds during last term. Pól O Dubhláin, who was senior prefect, held the Connacht Championship in the 100 and 220 yards from the previous season's colleges finals. But that was another country as far as the experts in the big smoke of Leinster Colleges athletics were concerned.

We must have been a strange sight in the Iveagh Grounds on the day of the finals, speaking Irish in a variety of accents but as cocky as hell for we had a firm belief in Pól's ability to win. The fact that he was looked up to by everyone in the school, because of his gentleness combined with a strict sense of fair-play, may have clouded our judgement but when he won the 100 yards we felt that Coláiste Einde had been put on the athletic map.

So did the men from the big smoke for they could be heard wondering aloud about the school's location. When Pól won the 220 we went wild and even our president, Dr Donncha O hEidhin, was seen to smile and dance a discreet jig.

Later on, one of our number heard a spectator explain to his colleague that, perhaps because of lack of space in the newspapers due to rationing of newsprint, the country had not been told that Pearse's old school in Rathfarnham had been opened up again.

Paul Dolan continued to develop as a sprinter and represented Ireland in the London and Helsinki Olympics as well as at many international competitions. He was a very tense runner, who suffered terribly from stomach nerves before races — a trait that was at variance with his very placid nature but is common among performers in various activities other than athletic. Broadcasters, even very experienced ones, are known to suffer from attacks of what are known as "butterflies in the stomach" before "live" performances. Some of them worry if they feel too relaxed before a performance and maintain that the performance is never as sharp when the nerves are too steady before it.

We all shared in that triumph and it ended our spell in "exile" in Dublin on a very high note. The training college was opening again in September and some of our seniors, including Paul, were sitting their Leaving Certificate examinations and would not be with us in Galway when we took possession of Coláiste Einde from the army.

One of the reasons why our president has not been conspicuous in this account, so far, is that he spent a lot of time haunting the Departments of Education and Defence in a constant effort to get his college back. He regarded its occupation by the military as a personal affront and a slight to his authority. He also swooped on the building occasionally and listed all the scars and disfigurements he noted since his last spot-check and brought these to the attention of the relevant authorities. The poor man would surely turn in his grave if he could see the building today. It stands battered and weather-stained like a gigantic ball-alley against which a tribe of giants were in the habit of relieving their bladders.

4

For most of that first summer home from school I lazed, fished a little from the rocks below our house, learned to play the melodeon after a fashion and began to borrow books from Dr O'Brien. Lazing came naturally to me and I have always retained a capacity to retire into myself and put my mind in neutral until boredom forces me to release whatever energy I may have conserved. Aran Islanders, as Máirtín O Cadhain and others have noted, can almost blend into the physical background, remaining completely still and remote from all that is active in their vicinity.

Once we had a parish priest who delighted in farming the parochial smallholding (which had previously belonged to the Church of Ireland rector before he emigrated to Ireland for want of a flock) and buying and selling cattle. One summer's day he was working furiously, trying to save a field of hay before the threatening rain turned it into a sodden mess. Every time he looked up from his work towards the darkening sky his eyes were offended by the sight of a young man from the village, stretched full length on the coping stones of a wall overlooking the priest's meadow, his cap pulled down over his eyes, motionless.

When the first light drops of rain blew in from the Atlantic to let the parish priest know that his furious labours were in vain, he dropped the rake, ran to the far end of the meadow and shouted to the figure on the wall, "And just what are you doing there?"

The recumbent one removed his cap, heaved himself up on his elbow and cheerfully replied, "Oh, hello, Father! I'm just waiting for the tide."

This perfectly reasonable fisherman's explanation infuriated the parish priest even more than the spectacle of sloth and he shouted back, "As far as I can make out this whole bloody island is waiting for the tide," and returned to his futile labour, defeated.

From our own front door I could observe the ebb and flow of the tide and all comings and goings in Galway Bay and beyond. I could view the coast from the mouth of the Shannon (with Mount Brandon in the background), up the length of Clare, past Doonbeg, Mal Bay, Hag's Head, the Cliffs of Moher and on to Black Head. Then you picked up the white-faced sand dunes at Bearna, across the mouth of the inner bay, and followed the Connemara shore, past Casla and Great Man's bay, past Golam Head, on to Carna and the little islands away to the west. The Connemara coast lay low but inland the land rose gradually to the rugged splendour of the Twelve Bens.

It was a splendid prospect when the weather was fine and the silver and indigo sea to the north of us was dotted with Connemara hookers, black-hulled and brown-sailed, carrying turf to the islands and Kinvara, or returning home light. We learned to recognise the different craft at great distances by various distinguishing marks: the colour of a jib, a stripe of paint along the gunwale or a patch on a mainsail.

When they arrived at the pier the bargaining began with the men who came to meet them, tie the ropes and pass disparaging remarks about the quality of the turf. To raise the price of a boatload by even half a crown was a breach of the social code but, nevertheless, it seemed to happen regularly every year.

I date part of my growth to manhood from the day I was sent to buy the turf. It was an easy task, for my father, who was away from home, dealt regularly with the same boatman, Peadar Choilm Mhóir from Sruthán. But part of the ritual consisted in taking the boatman and his helper for a drink to McDonough's pub overlooking the harbour: the customer stood the drinks first and the boatman returned the bargain-sealing treat.

The fact that I was only drinking lemonade and that I regarded a pint of porter as a wholly repellent drink, reminiscent of the cascara we were given to loosen our bowels, did nothing to diminish the feeling that I was now, in the Irish phrase, "ins na fir".

At night the prospect from our door was uniformly black but for the lights that shone in various densities along the coastline and the other little lights that flashed at intervals from Slyne Head, Black Head, Straw Island and Loop Head lighthouses. They were the friendliest lights of all.

On a stormy day the mainland almost vanished in a grey blanket and every breaker along our shore and out to sea as far as The Great Breaker – almost half way to Connemara – showed its lurking danger in white-maned waves and we looked down the bay, if it was a sailing day, and said to each other, "No fear of her sailing today".

We owned no land, thank God, and my brother Eanna and myself spent a lot of time avoiding what little labour was required of us in our vegetable garden, to the great disappointment of my mother who would have attempted to grow plants at the South Pole. Whenever she voiced her exasperation with her sons' reluctance to weed a patch of carrots, the listener always replied, "That's the way, God help us, but sure they will have the books."

My father, the son of a small farmer, also avoided the garden except when under extreme pressure. He was much happier in the company of some old man who could add something to his ever-increasing store of local history and folklore, much of which my mother, labouring alone to make flowers and shrubs grow on what had been bare crags a few years previously, regarded as disguised gossip.

My mother was very fond of music and was happy to see me learn to play the melodeon, although she would scarcely have approved of my motive had she been aware of it. She played it herself, from time to time, and said it restored tranquillity when she was worried or depressed. My Aunt Annie's daughter, Alice, who came to live with us after her mother's death and remained ever since an older sister to me, played it well and taught me my first dance tunes. But I left her also in ignorance of my truly mercenary motives.

I had observed that melodeon-players were invited everywhere: to dances in houses, weddings, and parties for those going to America or home on holidays. They were fed, foddered and generally pampered, for without them the merriment would be dependent on a hand-wound gramophone and a repetition of unsuitable dance music on discs that had to be changed every three minutes.

Not that the melodeon players were free from failings. They had a reputation for being temperamental, for taking offence and departing early with their instrument, or else taking a fancy to some girl and complaining that there was nobody to relieve them of their tiresome task. There was also a danger of their drinking too much and getting over-tired and losing rhythm and becoming obstreperous if anyone complained.

As I was then a strict Pioneer, a proven pugilistic failure, a non-dancer and far too shy to make up to a girl in public, I came to the conclusion that a future as a dependable melodeon-player lay ahead of me. I was right, too, and for a few years I was in demand in the nearby villages. But gradually I started to slide down the same well-lubricated slope that almost all melodeon-players descended, arriving eventually in the relegation area on my backside. But it was fun while it lasted.

At this stage of my life as a reader I had exhausted the family library, ending with the Masterpiece Library's *One Thousand of the World's Best Stories*, in I forget how many volumes, and drawing the line at Butler's *Lives of the Saints* in eight.

These collections, which filled the shelves in many a

teacher's home, included the complete works of Dickens, the collected works of P.H. Pearse, Cassell's Books of Knowledge and many others. We seemed to have most of them, for the poor devils who came to sell them on commission for publishing companies in Dublin and London were, almost without exception, school teachers who had been fired for one reason or another: usually it was the one reason and it was writ large upon their raw, red faces and rheumy eyes.

One of them entered my father's classroom most dramatically one day during catechism class. He had a mane of white hair and although it was not far short of Christmas, wore only a light battered suit and an open neck shirt. He had obviously repaired the damage done by the previous night's excesses for he threw open the door and roared, "God bless all here! Are you the Principal? It was Séamuisín O hAodha, the bastard, that put me on the road."

Séamus O hAodha was a divisional inspector and a poet of sorts in the Irish language. He once came to our school and we found him mild, if a trifle over-sweet and my mother noticed that when he smiled his eyes did not smile. In those days something approaching open warfare existed between teachers, inspectors and school managers who were almost always parish priests. Now, whenever I see Séamus O hAodha's name, I immediately think of that poor man with his wild mane of hair, reeking of whiskey, standing in Kilronan school and how utterly inconceivable I would have found then any suggestion that a little more than a decade later I might find myself flogging unwanted books to good-natured teachers.

It was from this man that we acquired Butler's *Lives of the Saints*, all other items on his list having already been purchased from the other poor derelicts who had preceded him. The subsequent history of those beautifully-bound tomes is interesting. My father lent them to the local religious maniac, partly in the hope that they would never come back, but this one was a genuine religious maniac and he returned them, one by one, as soon as he had finished reading them.

Then an excessively reflective man, in another village, came to a strange conclusion after much reading and thought. He concluded that scientists and geographers had failed to see that as a result of the Panama Canal being opened, the Gulf Stream would flow into the Pacific Ocean and another ice age would occur in northern Europe. He took to his bed to await this eventuality and rapidly ran out of reading matter.

As soon as we heard the news we rushed Butler's *Lives of the Saints* to his bedside and impressed on him that they would last a long time if taken infrequently and in small doses. But the man realised, after three or four years in bed, that he had calculated wrongly, got up, returned the books and lived to be a ripe old age. The eight volumes were finally marooned on Inis Mór when my parents sold the house and moved to the mainland.

Our doctor, Jim O'Brien, had a house full of books which he lent to certain people provided they returned them in time and in good condition. He had his own way of impressing this fact on borrowers. He would say, "I had another book now that I'm sure you'd enjoy but what do you call that little spy fella, that used to go to communion every morning? I forget his name but he stole the bloody book and I wouldn't mind so much but it's out of print. You can't be too careful."

Dr O'Brien was a publican as well as being our dispensary doctor, having inherited the pub, some house property, land and a tidy sum of money from his mother who died in the mid-thirties. She was a formidable lady, by all accounts — a first cousin of Máirtín Mór McDonough, who opened a shop in Kilronan and made a small fortune during the fishing boom in the first two decades of the century. Her husband, John O'Brien, came from Connemara and died while still a young man. All I ever heard said of him was that he was a quiet, decent man.

Jim O'Brien was sent to school in St Jarlath's and afterwards to Blackrock College, for his mother was determined that he was to be a doctor. Once, when I passed some comment on the harshness of life in boarding school, he told me some stories of life in Jarlath's and Blackrock, at the turn of the century, that made a deep impression on me and made Coláiste Einde seem like a first-class hotel.

Smoking was strictly forbidden and the smokers took to chewing tobacco which was also forbidden. Fresh plugs of tobacco were hidden in secret crevices in the walls and chewing took place at the back of the ball-alley.

The "chews" were drained of saliva and secreted inside the front fold of the cap, over the peak; every now and then boys were corralled in a room and their caps searched. The quick thinkers hurled their "chews" out of the windows, as the punishment for being "caught in possession" was a severe hammering with an ash plant. After one of these raids took place there was a great stampede to retrieve the jettisoned "chews", for there seemed to be a disgusting lack of squeamishness about chewing another student's masticated tobacco.

Like many another good medical practitioner of his day, Dr O'Brien took a dozen years to qualify. This was far from being due to lack of intelligence: rather to a surfeit of sensitivity, an inability to regurgitate information adequately in examinations and a chronic difficulty with surgery. I also gathered that he was in no particular hurry to qualify. He loved Dublin and frequented all the pubs where he could observe all that was interesting in life, high and low. When Brendan Behan came to Aran he was bowled over by the doctor's minute knowledge of the city. There was plenty of money at home to support him and if he did make a conscious decision to extend his stay he was wiser than he may have imagined at the time. Never again in his long life did he enjoy such complete freedom and he carried the Dublin of Joyce's *Ulysses* around in his head for the rest of his days.

I was not alone in thinking that Jim O'Brien would have been better suited to a profession other than the one chosen for him by his mother. He must have spent a lot of time in art galleries during his years in Dublin for he amassed a huge collection of books on art and artists. Seán Keating and Charles Lamb, who painted in Aran and who got to know the doctor, were impressed by his knowledge and by his critical eye. Elizabeth Rivers, who spent some years in Inis Mór, and as well as painting and drawing also wrote a quaint book about the island, was convinced that Jim O'Brien could have been a first-class critic. For a quiet and rather shy man his enthusiasms were very infectious and although I am close to being a visual illiterate, he managed to transmit to me his passion for Holman Hunt and the Pre-Raphaelites.

Both Charles Lamb and my Uncle Liam begged him to sell the pub and the houses, let the land and go to live in Paris, something he sometimes spoke diffidently of doing. Liam went so far as to draw up a detailed estimate of annual expenditure, on the counter of the pub one day, including provision for the services of a housekeeper. The doctor moved around the shop chuckling to himself, "Would you get a young housekeeper for that kind of money now, Liam? Ha? I'd probably end as some sort of a pox-doctor. Ha?" They both realised it was a sort of charade.

After a short period doing locum in Leenane and parts of Mayo he had come to Aran. While in Leenane he was called to treat Sir Henry Rider Haggard's valet for burns, his master having thrown a pot of coffee at him while in one of his rages; and in Mayo he had a fierce confrontation with the famous Father Ned Lavelle. But in Aran he spent most of his long life living alone in a huge cavern of two connected houses, with only a dog for company. Of course he had his books, hundreds and hundreds of them, stacked in the most unlikely places. He also had his patients, and his customers, whenever he chose to open his extraordinary pub.

A vivid picture of the pub's unique disorder may be found in Liam's short story "Mearbhall" ("The Fanatic" in the English version) but little of the doctor is to be found in the character of the tavern keeper (based on a publican encountered when travelling in west Mayo with Earnán O Máille in 1947), apart from the description of his eyes:

"They were like a woman's eyes soft and gentle and amorous. It was quite impossible to identify their colour in that dark room. They seemed to be a mixture of brown and grey and green, like the little smooth multi-coloured stones that lie at the bottom of a swiftly-running mountain torrent on whose surface the bright rays of the sun are dancing."

I was fascinated by the relationship between my uncle and the doctor. Each discussed the other with me without finding it necessary to censor his thoughts. Liam realised that the doctor had the genuine creative instinct and was impatient with him for not having found an outlet for it, except for his wonderful stories and his eccentric way of life.

It was from Dr O'Brien he heard the stories on which he based "The Oar", "The Strange Disease", "Blood Lust", "The Mountain Tavern" and some of the nature stories. But the doctor resented having the characters of the doctors in *The House of Gold* and *Skerret* based, however loosely, on himself. He never mentioned *The House of Gold* to Liam, partly because it was based on his cousins, the McDonoughs of Galway. But he did tell me that he once brought up the matter of Dr Melia in *Skerret* and that Liam's reply was, "Jesus, Jim, didn't I pack you off to the States with a fine young woman". This may indeed have been Liam's wish for his friend expressed in *Skerret* but there are limits to such speculation.

I could see another aspect of Dr O'Brien's situation in Aran, which his façade of independence could not hide. The terrible respectability of his mother's people, as well as the conventional behaviour expected of a member of his profession in the employment of Galway County Council, put a curb on both his wish for independence and his eccentricity. But I also could see that Liam's solution to most problems, taking the shortest and quickest route in the opposite direction, would eventually lead to the dead being left to bury the dead. I tried it myself later and can vouch that it does not work in the end.

In 1940, when I was serving on the altar for a mission given by the Redemptorist fathers, who had come to the island to give the souls of the faithful a major refit, one of my tasks at evening devotions was to ring the bell for "the sinners of the parish who are not attending the mission", while the congregation knelt and prayed for them. One of the three was the doctor and he conceded on the third night. I can still see him walking slowly down the back road to the church, wearing the good suit which he only wore when on a rare holiday on the mainland. It saddened me for he did not really want to go and this proved that he was not really independent at all, despite his wealth. He could not even crack a joke with the men who lay against the walls, smoking and waiting for the summoning bell, as Séimín O Cualáin had done the previous night.

Séimín had chased one of the Redemptorists away from his door with a pitchfork, the cleric being unaware that he had been on a tear and was in no mood to discuss his absence from the mission. The following day he came down the road, aware that all eyes were on him, and when he came near the men he raised his hands over his head and said, "Well, sure even poor Leopold of the Belgians had to surrender honourably in the face of superior forces."

One of the first books the doctor gave me was *Moby Dick*, one of his own particular favourites. I found it heavy going and returned it to him, unfinished, a few days before I went back to school. He told me to try again, that it was well worth the effort, and surprised me by saying that I could take it away to school and come back and talk to him about it at Christmas.

Again, I got entangled in the opening chapters, and although I could have told a lie and said I enjoyed it greatly, I knew him well enough to know that he was capable of putting my false enthusiasm to the test. On Christmas Eve my mother had a bad headache and requested tablets from the doctor but he was away in Inis Meáin attending a difficult birth. Late in the evening we heard he had come back in a currach and I went down to his house on the bicycle with *Moby Dick* in my pocket.

He was in the kitchen, cooking his supper, still wearing his sodden clothes. After he had got some tablets for my mother, I returned the book and confessed that it had defeated me for the second time. He gave me one of his quizzical looks over the top of his heavy glasses.

"You couldn't get it? Ha! Isn't that a good one now? Most peculiar. Maybe you're not going the right way about it. Come into the kitchen for a minute: I won't keep you long."

He had potatoes boiling in a pot and a piece of smoked conger eel simmering in a pan of milk and onions: the traditional Christmas Eve "first supper" of fish and potatoes. The kitchen looked as if it had not been tidied since old Mrs O'Brien died. His black and white dog, Rex, lay snoring in the middle of a heap of apples on a sheet under the table.

Waking the dog up with a kick, he opened the book and turning to the chapter on "The Whiteness of the Whale" read extracts and gave explanations while testing the potatoes and cooking the conger eel. The secret of *Moby Dick* was to understand what it was really all about and the key was in this chapter. He may have been just a good psychologist but in my case it worked and I read the book again. Some years later I really began to understand and I have been re-reading the book ever since.

The excitement of returning to the real Coláiste Einde was quickly dampened by the fact that we only occupied half the building: the other half was still an army hospital and remained so until the end of that school year. This meant that no new students were taken in, the year's intake going to Baile Mhúirne which meant an O'Sullivan Beara-type trek, six times a year, for the Donegal contingent. That in turn affected our football teams, as it meant fielding a senior and a junior team out of our total of 44 pupils in second, third and fourth years.

Worse still, it had a terrible effect on Dr O hEidhin's temper. Exile in Drumcondra was nothing compared to being in a partitioned building with the odious occupiers under his eyes all the time. Every time his eyes lit on the many indentations left by army beds on the beautiful rubberoid floors, every time our temporary kitchens broke down and, worst of all, every time he heard the sound of the harmonium from our occupied oratory, his forehead corrugated in deep wrinkles and wise students kept their weather eyes open.

Strict rules were laid down forbidding even the most superficial contact with army personnel under pain of the Coláiste Einde equivalent of capital punishment.

One night, shortly after the beginning of first term, I was summoned from the temporary study hall to the President's office. I was almost sure I had done nothing wrong, and had therefore nothing to fear, but with Dr O hEidhin you were never completely sure. He invented thought police years before the idea entered George Orwell's mind and took the precaution of limiting membership to himself.

He was sitting behind his desk and he stared at me for a while as if he had forgotten why he had summoned me from my proper place in the study hall. He was a small, bald-headed man with white skin and very dark facial hair which gave his jaws a bluish tinge towards evening. His eyebrows were black and very pronounced and when he was out of sorts he looked like a dyspeptic owl who had lost more than a few days' sleep.

"You have a relative," he said at last, taking off his glasses and rubbing his eyes with the back of his hand. "A relative," he repeated, just as I was preparing myself for news of a death in the family, "who does not understand the rules of this college."

This was nothing as simple and straightforward as a death: this conundrum clearly meant trouble. He leant forward and began to swing his glasses in front of me as if trying to mesmerise me.

"This man . . . this person . . . this relative . . . came in here tonight and walked along the corridor . . . smelling . . . smelling . . . smelling of drink, boy, and asking to see you. Do you understand?"

He lay back in the chair, replaced his glasses and delivered the punch line: "This person . . . who says he is a relative of yours . . . came from over there. He is a . . . soldier!"

It seems that this relative, whose name he did not choose to give for another three minutes, was malingering in hospital and came over, unannounced and uninvited to see me, full of family feeling and Guinness in unequal proportions, according to Dr O hEidhin. He was wandering along the corridor in hospital garb when he literally bumped into the President and ordered him jovially to fetch his kinsman for a little chat. Everything else that happened I can only guess, for Dr O hEidhin said no more and my relative had no memory at all of his crossing of the Salthill Wall. But I had to write a letter to him, there and then, and give it to the President for instant delivery by hand, instructing my relative in the rules of the College. It was my first, but not my last, audience with Dr O hEidhin.

Luckily, he did not teach us, nor indeed did he ever but once, as I recall, take any active part in our extra-curricular activities. A group of us who had entered a verse-speaking competition in Feis Cheoil an Iarthair, more for the love of an evening's freedom and an opportunity to chat up the girls from the Dominican, Mercy and Presentation convents than out of devotion to poetry, received some coaching from Dr O hEidhin. He had a beautiful voice and the graceful walk of a dancer but he had no understanding at all of how to deal with growing boys, apart from laying down endless rules and enforcing them rigorously.

Every Sunday morning he came into study, during the time allowed for letter writing to approved addresses, and lectured us. The occasion seemed to cause him greater pain and discomfort than it caused us. He would ascend the high chair behind the desk that dominated the study and call us to order: "A bhuachaillí". He would remove his biretta and his glasses and grimace for some time before replacing them. He would then launch into a series of complaints which ranged from deficient table manners, and misdemeanours like dropping laundry bags over the banisters instead of carrying them down and placing them in the basket and rubbing the walls of the corridors with our elbows, to various transgressions of rules concerning the showers and toilets.

Sometimes he was unintentionally hilarious. Once he gave a lecture on the subject of a polish tin, the lid of which had blocked a toilet. He wondered aloud and at length on the reasons which could provoke such a senseless act in an institution so well stocked with all necessary toilet requisites. As various Rabelaisian conjectures were going through most minds in the audience, the hall was soon simmering with suppressed snorts of laughter for which no real outlet could be found. A burst of ribald laughter would see our few little privileges — like going to the barber's without having a hair inspection — vanish in a blast of humourless anger.

Life in Coláiste Einde was much the same as it was in any other boarding school of the period, with a few important differences. We had no day-pupils and therefore no constant contact with the outside world except through our teachers. We were better fed than most, in those lean post-war years, for the Department contracted for supplies and both Dr O hEidhin and the Matron supervised rigorously. Our teachers, who were also appointed by the state, were excellent and our facilities first-class. Whenever we visited other colleges we saw how unfavourably they contrasted with our own which was kept in gleaming condition by the Board of Works. We had a good library, music rooms and a little theatre and I must admit that most of my memories of these years are very happy ones.

Yet, having tasted a good deal of freedom in Dublin, the gradual restriction on even short visits to the world outside our granite walls became irksome, particularly because there seemed to be no good reason for it and, if there was, nobody took the trouble to explain it to us. But then, blind obedience to the most mindless of rules seemed to be considered the hallmark of the upstanding young Christian at that time and for years afterwards.

Not that we spent all that much time brooding. Dr O hEidhin's defenders among us maintained that he was not altogether to blame for our long periods of incarceration. The fault lay with Dr Michael Browne, Bishop of Galway, who was said to resent the presence of a college in his diocese which was largely outside his control. That was why we had had so much freedom in Dublin, they argued, and was it not significant that he never visited the college although he lived a mere half mile away, down the slope of Taylor's Hill?

Nobody knew the answer and looking back on it now, the restriction on going into Galway — to the cinema, Taibhdhearc na Gaillimhe and the few gaelic matches of interest — affected us but occasionally. But when it did, gloom, irritability and homesickness spread through the school and poisoned the atmosphere. The urge to get out became an obsession.

When I was at sea in later life I experienced the same querulous, nasty atmosphere on board when we were coming to the end of a trip. Everyone seemed to get on everyone else's nerves and the man who walked down one side of the deck, as you walked up the other, seemed to be crowding you.

When I went to UCG, I told a student who had been in St Jarlath's that I began to play football seriously at school so as to travel away with the team. A trip to Tuam was welcome while going to Roscommon was like going abroad. It was rather like the man from our island who had never been to Galway and was reputed to have said, "Now, if I could even get TB I would be sent there." The other student said that when he was going away for the first time an experienced local told him to start swotting his football immediately. "The footballers get food," he was told, "The rest have to get by on the clippings of tin cans."

What really happened in my case was that an tAthair O Laoi, who was in charge of games, and Máirtín Mac Dónaill, who was the best footballer in our class, convinced me that the honour of the school depended on the fit and willing developing whatever footballing talent God gave them. For me that meant leaving a snug berth in goal and moving into the right corner of the full back line.

At first I hated being out of goal and involved in constant bodily contact — which is another way of saying that I was something of a physical coward. Then, like the cowardly winger, Regan, in the O'Flaherty short story, "The Wing Three-Quarter", I found that fear departed when I got thumped by another player, particularly if I thought it an unfair assault. After that I never considered the danger of injury, and the idea of playing to the best of my ability for the honour of the school sustained my enthusiasm for a couple of years.

As I relied on speed to get me out of tight corners and as I was lightly built, I was rarely involved in tough physical buffeting. Only once was I spoken to by a referee, when I lost my temper with a persistent jersey-puller and took the law into my own hands by charging into him, knees first. I got off with a warning but was severely lectured the following day in class by an tAthair O Laoi who was an admirer of spirited play but drew the line firmly at dirty play and left us in no doubt at all on the matter.

Many years later when I read Dr C.S. Andrews' autobiography, *Dublin Made Me*, I was reminded of that incident in my own short career in schools football by the following passage, in which Tod Andrews describes how as a soccer man and cricket follower he was forced to play gaelic football in jail as foreign games were banned:

The league matches were of a high standard as the teams were studded with All-Ireland players from different counties. The games were very tough. I was introduced to what must be the most infuriating foul in any code of football. When you are about to jump, with arms extended to take a ball out of the air, you find your feet are stuck to the ground. Someone has hung on to the tail of your jersey. An almost murderous feeling of exasperation overwhelmed me when that happened. I could not resist lashing out with my fists; hence I developed a reputation for being a very rough player.

When I went home that summer, after the Intermediate Certificate examination, I called in to Dr O'Brien to borrow books and we talked of school. I told him that I was about to take up football seriously as we would be trying to pick a senior team out of less than thirty boys, next term, and a junior team out of much less, combined with whatever talent came in with the first years. Handball was the Doctor's favourite game and I was later to find it the most satisfying game of all, but for the moment my enthusiasm was for football.

Although we were small in numbers the school ended the football season in a blaze of glory when two of our players, Diarmuid O Súileabháin from Kerry and Proinsias O Dónaill from Donegal, were chosen on a Connacht Colleges team in the company of stars like Seán Purcell, Jack Mangan, Frank Stockwell, Peter Solan, Mick Flanagan and many others.

They beat Leinster in the final in Tuam and although we did not travel we were allowed to listen to the radio commentary. We were proud to hear the commentator, Seán O Síocháin, say more than once in the course of a great game, "Is íontach an fear cúil an Súileabhánach" (O'Sullivan is a great back). But as well as being proud we were now convinced that excellence did not depend on numbers.

For some years the provincial championships, in hurling and football, were run in tandem with the individual colleges championship, the Hogan Cups. It seems to me a pity that the interprovincial competition was afterwards abandoned for it did give an opportunity to great footballers from smaller colleges, like Coláiste Einde, to display their skills in the company of the best players from the larger colleges. Representing the province at that age could mean far more to a player than being chosen to play in the Railway Cup competition later on.

Dr O'Brien proved equal to my latest enthusiasm. He began to rummage around the shop, muttering to himself and to me about a book he had picked up from a barrow on the Dublin quays, if he could only find it, and after rooting under barrels and behind bottles produced a little green-covered book which he told me I could keep. This rare offer startled me even more than the sight of *How to Play Gaelic Football* by Dick Fitzgerald, the first book on gaelic games I ever possessed.

Dick Fitzgerald played for Kerry in the All-Irelands of 1903, '04, '05, '08 and '09 and captained the team in the All-Irelands of 1913, '14 and '15, as well as captaining teams in various jails during the War of Independence. He is regarded by those who saw him play, or played against him, as one of the greatest of all time. This is how he saw the game a year after the 15-a-side rule had been introduced in 1913:

Gaelic football of the present day is a scientific game. It is necessary to lay this down at the very beginning, because some people have got an idea into their heads that the game is unscientific, and they have no scruple about saying so.

There was a time, indeed, when the game was anything but a scientific exposition. This was the case some twenty years ago, when the rough-and-tumble and go-for-the-man obtained. Then it was rather a trial of strength and endurance than an exhibition of skill. But all that is gone long since. Even as far back as the nineties, when as many as twenty-one men a side played, there was not wanting signs of development on the scientific side. Later on, when the game was confined to seventeen players a side, it became more and more a trial of skill, as in the famous Kerry v. Kildare matches, and, finally, when the number was reduced to fifteen a side, Science became the order of the day.

Can anyone say that Gaelic Football is unscientific since the memorable encounters between Kerry and Louth in May and June, 1913? Some forty thousand people witnessed each of these strenuous tussles for supremacy, and it has been said on all sides that never in the history of outdoor games in Ireland have people gone home so well pleased with what they saw. Assuredly no one would be found foolish enough who can now maintain that our National Football Game is not scientific.

The fact is that, given two well-trained teams coming from an area where there has been a tradition of good Gaelic football, and given fair weather conditions for the playing of the match, the game is bound to be most interesting to watch, and the better exponents of the science of the game are nearly always sure to come out on top.

In a certain sense, Gaelic Football of the present day is more scientific than any existing football game. In other forms of football, such is the constitution of the rules governing them, there is very often too much of the element of luck. In the native game, however, there is no such preponderance of luck, as the results prove, and this is to be accounted for by the fact that the rules provide the two kinds of score, viz., the Point as well as the Goal.

We cannot help dwelling upon one or two other attractive features of the Gaelic Code. Everybody knows that the tendency of outdoor games of the present day is to reduce the individual player to the level of a mere automaton. In a manner, the individual in the modern game is a disadvantage to his side, if his individuality asserts itself strongly — so strongly, at least, that he tends to be too much of an individualist and too little of the mere machine. How dry is the description one often gets of those great matches, in which perfect combination alone is the only thing commended! In them there is no hero — no great individual standing out from the whole field. If he did stand out, he would cease to be a machine, and his usefulness to his side would cease likewise.

Gaelic Football fortunately does not tend in the direction of reducing its players to the mere machine level. True it is that combination — and combination of a sufficiently high standard — is much prized. Each player is taught to see the advantage of combining with everybody else on his side, and of playing at all times unselfishly. But, such is the genius of the game itself, that while combination will always be prominent, the brilliant individual gets his opportunities time out of mind, with the result that, after the match is over, you will generally have a hero or two carried enthusiastically off the field on the shoulders of their admirers.

Then, too, Gaelic Football is what may be called a natural football game. There is no incentive in it towards rough play. One player can hamper or impede another in one way, and only one way, and that by means of the shoulder. Hence it is that severe tackling, rough handling, and all forms of tripping are banned.

Truly there is no artificiality about our game. There is no such thing as the artificial "forward", "off-side", "knock-on" etc., rules, hedging the player about in all his movements. When men are bound down by almost impossible restrictions, such as those just mentioned, it is only very highly trained machines that can adapt themselves to the playing of a game under such conditions. No wonder it is that professionalism has come so much into modern outdoor games, which require the players of them to devote practically all their time to learn how to play, and consequently to make their living thereby.

It is to be hoped that Gaelic Football will always remain as natural a game as it is today; and accordingly we trust that, while it will ever be developing on the scientific side, it may never become the possession of the professional player.

A lot of what Fitzgerald wrote went over my head and the only practical knowledge I gained from reading his book was the importance he placed on ball control on the ground: dribbling the ball and playing it off the ground with the foot, in defence and in attack. But at last I had something Irish to add to the pile of books and magazines on sports of all kinds I had accumulated since inheriting Roger Hammond's collection.

About the author I knew little, except that his life ended tragically in 1930 and that the fine stadium in Killarney is named in his honour. Later I learned that in Kerry, during his lifetime, he was known simply as "Dickeen".

5

It was at this time also that a change came over the pattern of my summer holidays. Clare began to lose some of its attraction. I was growing up and well able to give a hand with the daily chores, in contrast with previous summers when I used to head off to Miltown every morning on my bicycle to sit and absorb the news of the day in O'Halloran's tailoring establishment, or play with the boys on the Fair Green, coming home by Spanish Point and Quilty when the pangs of hunger finally moved me.

At first I enjoyed the work: taking the milk to the creamery and then driving to the bog with the pony and cart to bring the turf out to the roadside, or going to the meadow to help save the hay. I felt I was doing a man's work, and the conversation of the young men at the creamery at Coore in the mornings did help to strengthen the illusion of manliness in the most obvious respect.

But that feeling quickly dissipated. The routine of farm work and particularly the tyranny of the cows and their swelling udders soon taught me the reality of the small dairy farmer's life. It came as no surprise to me, in later life, that their most constant critics in the cities and towns showed such a marked reluctance to pack up their unhealthy, heavily-taxed jobs and take up what they choose to portray as a cossetted and over-protected way of life. Soon I was spending less time on the farm and a lot more fishing in a currach with my cousins in Mainistir, just below our house.

During the summer of 1945, my father, who was an energetic cyclist, suggested that we take a spin through east Galway and the Midlands and go to the All-Ireland hurling semi-final between Galway and Kilkenny, in Birr, on the last Sunday in July. I should point out that during the war years, and for many years afterwards, the bicycle was the sole means of covering long distances in rural Ireland and people thought nothing of cycling fifty or sixty miles to a big match. The absence of heavy traffic and the company of hundreds of fellow-cyclists helped to ease the hardship.

The previous year we arrived in Ennis, on our way from Galway to Miltown, the day after the hurling semi-final between Galway and Cork. The sole topic of conversation in the town seemed to be the disputed point which won the game for Cork. Some maintained that the referee had blown for a Cork free, before the point was scored. The referee said he had not blown but had allowed Cork the advantage.

Down the years the Galway hurlers seemed to have had little luck with referees, regardless of where they came from. I do seem to recollect a Tipperary referee who had to take to his heels and to his fields, the night after he had refereed a match, when he was approached by a party of Galwaymen, in a car, who wished to test the thickness of his cranium with the curved wooden objects they were carrying. But the referee in 1944 was a Clareman and Galway have had no luck at all with Clare referees.

In 1944 Cork were about to complete their fourth All-Ireland victory in a row and although they had to play without Jack Lynch and John Quirke, Galway were not expected to trouble them. It was the talk, the subsequent objection and the fact that Cork went on to thrash Dublin in the final that really awakened my interest in the Galway hurling team. In time it almost became an obsession.

Although I never hurled in any real competitive sense, an tAthair O Laoi did his best to foster the game in Coláiste Einde, against insurmountable difficulties. He came from Michael Cusack's parish of Carron and was a fine footballer, hurler and handball player. Such was the variety of talents within our small band of students that two of them, Eoghan O Cadhain from Moycullen and Pádraig O Fallúin from Roscrea, played for the Connacht Colleges hurling team, and although they did not have the same success as their football-playing classmates, they did play in Croke Park. They also did their best to share their skills with those of us who were interested.

An tAthair O Laoi ordered a batch of hurleys and never before, or since, have I seen such a splintering of timbers as took place on the evening of their arrival on our pitch. It was quite terrifying while it lasted and amazing that all who took part lived to tell the tale.

Many years afterwards, when the film *Christy Ring* was being shot in Cork, a member of the crew who had never handled a hurley, and who regarded hurling as a very dangerous game, asked Christy if he was ever afraid on the field. Christy smiled the bleak smile that signalled disapproval or contempt and said, "Only when I'm playing against bad hurlers."

That much I learned in school and although the honourable experiment failed, it lasted long enough to give me an insight into the skills of the game and proved that tuition at an early age could impart them to a novice, but that only in competitive contest against skilful hurlers, while coached by an expert, could the game be mastered by someone who had not grown up with it. I also remember that some of our more enthusiastic footballers were very dismissive of an tAthair O Laoi's attempt to broaden our experience. They saw it as a danger to our meagre human resources and therefore a threat to football. That may have been the most important lesson, for it is at the root of the GAA's practical attitude to the game that is ritualistically referred to as the brightest jewel in the organisation's crown, which it is, but it is not treated accordingly.

Personally, the attempt to promote hurling in Coláiste Einde cultivated an interest that increased with the passage of time and gave me a practical insight which could never have been gained from the sidelines.

So, in 1945, my father and I set out from Galway on a fine Saturday morning, cycling through Oranmore, Craughwell, Loughrea, Killimor and into Portumna, where we spent the night. It was the longest spell I had ever spent in the saddle but although I went out like a light when I hit the pillow, I felt no great fatigue.

In fact I was so energetic the following morning, heading across the Shannon to Birr, that I began to overtake and race up hills and my father warned me about burning up the energy which would be needed for the journey home. That did not trouble me at all. I foresaw the journey back to Galway as a long celebration, lit by bonfires and shortened by cheering crowds.

The day was fine and we got into the sidelines and I had my first view of hard championship hurling at close quarters. One has to be as close as possible to ground level and not too far from the players to appreciate the intensity as well as the skills of hurling. And for a long time it looked as if Galway's year had indeed come at last. They led for periods, once by seven points, but I was still too inexperienced to know that any lead that can be wiped away by two good strokes, or two bad mistakes in defence, is not a matter for confidence until the final whistle blows.

Kilkenny crept back and Galway began to show signs of panic — and lack of match practice, according to the knowledgeable ones around me. Kilkenny levelled the scores with time running out and the talk was of a replay and a different referee, of course. Then Kilkenny got another free and Jim Langton scored the winning point.

Even in my dismay I remember marvelling that his sleek, well-oiled hair showed not a strand out of place after an hour of furious hurling. Only when we had left Birr, heading back towards Portumna, with Galway city an unimaginable distance away to the west, did dark depression descend, aided by the doleful conversation of our fellow-travellers.

For it was during this painful journey that I first heard

of the curse that hung over the Galway hurling team, like that black cloud that appears over Clonmel every market day since the day Father Sheehy was hanged.

This curse, which must have been finally lifted on the first Sunday in September, 1980 — leaving all the real problems of the Galway senior hurling team intact — was attributed to a priest who was annoyed by some men he heard creeping out of his church before mass had ended. Seeing that they were members of the county hurling team, rushing to a match, he is said to have cursed the county team. For me, this was nothing unusual. I had heard people, and even houses, cursed most elaborately from the altar during clerical campaigns against the making and the sale of poitín.

But although I found the story easy to believe there seemed to be as many versions of the curse as there were locations for the original happening. I was told it happened in Castlegar ("On my solemn oath!"), Gort ("As sure as I'm standing here!"), Woodford ("May I be struck down dead if there's a word of a lie in it!") and more or less any hurling parish about twenty miles distant from where the teller of the tale resided.

Most versions of the story agreed on what the priest said: that while a player from the named parish was a member of the Galway team they would never win an All-Ireland, but would come as close to winning, at times, as the backsliders had come to hearing a full mass.

This story, which nobody really believed until events seemed to warrant some supernatural explanation, was being trotted out by every second cyclist coming home from Birr that night. I must say it gained a lot of credence in the years between 1944 and 1953, for reasons which will become clear later.

But for me the journey home ended in Loughrea where I almost fell off my bike, as an attack of fatigue and attendant sleepiness enveloped me. But even before I fell asleep in Moylan's Hotel, I told my father that never again would I travel a mile of road in support of those bewitched hurlers.

The following year we cycled from Galway to Birr on the Saturday before the semi-final with Cork, and woke on Sunday to find the rain coming down in heavy, grey sheets. There was not a breath of wind, and it was sultry. The day was well remembered in Birr because of the ton or so of sandwiches that went stale and mouldy for lack of custom and had to be thrown away.

The rain was so heavy that my father was tempted to listen to the match on the radio in the guest house where we stayed. I think he would have done so but for the constant whingeing of the man of the house about the decline and decay of Birr since the departure of the British Army from the barracks outside the town in 1922. Sitting in the rain and watching Galway getting hammered must have seemed preferable to listening to this particular tale of woe, for that is what we had to suffer instead.

It was a truly dreadful game. Galway only scored three points and were beaten by thirteen. Towards the end I was almost thankful for the torrent, for it helped conceal the tears of misery and disappointment. But despite the rain there were many cyclists on the road west that night, and as we sheltered from the heavy showers that followed the deluge, there was even more talk about the curse. I said very little. I remembered last year's vow and how silly I had been to break it. Now I was older, sadder and much wiser.

The following year we crept up on Birr from its southern flank, through Limerick, Nenagh and Roscrea. The weather was glorious, the farmers elated and Galway hearts were full of hope, for at last there came a sign that the luck of the hurlers had changed. For on 6 April, 1947, Connacht hurlers (Galwaymen all) had beaten Munster in the postponed Railway Cup final by seven points, having beaten Leinster by a point in the semi-final. This had to be their year . . . .

Again it was against Kilkenny, again the day was fine and the hurling fast, furious and, at times, reckless. Once, as some reporters noted, the ball travelled the length of the field from goal to goal, and back again, without touching the ground. It was touch and go, but Kilkenny got the winning point during the period of extra time, the length of which was debated for days afterwards. There was even a joke going the rounds at the time about the number of referees who dared not go to Galway Races.

The following day in Galway the arguments raged in shops, in pubs and along the streets. What was it about the Kilkenny jersey that seemed to mesmerise Galway, even when they seemed to have the upper hand? Similar arguments have been heard since. They were heard again after the final of 1979, even as far away as the pubs around Finsbury Park in London, where I viewed the game.

We abandoned the bikes that autumn in 1947 and took the excursion train to Dublin to see the final. This was partly due to the row kicked up by my brother Eanna, who was eleven and heartily sick of being treated like a baby in the family. No longer was he willing to put up with eye-witness accounts of matches and allied adventures from his brother. He wanted to see the real thing himself.

He got his way and he certainly picked the right year. As far as I am concerned, that final between Kilkenny and Cork was the best I have ever seen. It was memorable for many things, apart from Terry Leahy's dramatic winning point, scored from play seconds before the final whistle. For me, that did something to soften the blow of our own defeat in the semi-final while making me much more appreciative of the feelings of the Cork supporters in my vicinity who had been looking forward to better fortune in a replay. You learned all this from being there: feeling the elation and seeing the dejection.

From the lower reaches of Hill 16 I watched the Kilkenny newcomer, Peter Prendergast, the centre half back who had the task of minding Christy Ring. The papers said the result depended on this confrontation.

For the whole of the first half Prendergast must have scarcely blinked an eye, so closely did he stick to Ring. There was Irish sprint champion, Joe Kelly, at left corner forward for Cork, and the man who had to make sure he did not break away, Paddy Grace. There was Willie Murphy, the Cork corner back, known as "Long Puck" Murphy, whose prowess had been dramatised for us on radio by Michael O'Hehir.

Cork looked beaten at half-time and folklore has it that the team was lambasted in the dressing room. Be that as it may, changes were made that brought about a transformation. Ring was switched to one wing and Jack Lynch switched from mid-field to the other wing. The pressure was on Kilkenny now and I remember how Willie Murphy dropped the puck out near the Kilkenny twenty-one yard line, to increase that pressure.

This was the time when players used the one stick for all purposes. The Kilkenny goalkeeper, Jim Donegan, played a great game that day and he also used an ordinary hurley and not the modification of a half-door one sees used all too frequently today.

As the excitement rose the pressure from the crowd further up the Hill (there were over 60,000 at the match) drove us down against the sideline wall. Eanna complained that he could not see the field at all. He managed to climb up on my back and I held him there until we saw Terry Leahy's point go over and after that there was pandemonium and the final whistle.

On the way home on the extremely slow excursion train, everyone in the carriage, apart from myself, dozed off after we passed Athlone. I was suffering from a strange but severe headache and my scalp was sore to the touch. It took me some time to connect this with Eanna's enthusiastic pounding of my head with his fists, during the second half. I had scarcely noticed it at the time, my excitement being as great as his own.

Meanwhile, my resolution to play football seriously at school got an unexpected impetus when my Uncle Liam returned from America in 1946. He arrived to see me, unannounced as usual, appearing behind the goal during a practice match, with his regular greeting of "An tú atá ann?" (Is that you?). I was very embarrassed, standing there in my togs, breathless and sweaty, for he was accompanied by his daughter Peigín and two other ladies. But he was delighted. Everything about the college and about my present exertions fitted in perfectly with his current enthusiasms.

It was said in our family that my grandfather, Maidhc Mhicil Phádraig, was capable of changing his mind about people many times in the course of a single day. At breakfast, someone from another village would be mentioned and my grandfather would snort, "Don't mention that blackguard in this house. Running up to the back door of the police station at night like all his tribe." At supper that night some cautious member of the family, or a mischievous one, would say the acceptable thing about the same person. My grandfather would look at him in amazement and say: "What do you mean by calling that decent man a blackguard? I will not have a member of that honourable and patriotic family insulted in my presence."

Liam took after his father in that respect. But to complicate matters further, this idiosyncrasy did not mean that their attitudes to fundamental issues ever changed. In Liam's case it merely meant that you had to sound him out carefully before delivering a categorical statement — unless, of course, you were in the mood for a heated argument.

His involvement in the campaign for Irish neutrality, as well as the fact that he could not leave America for the duration of the war, seemed to have affected his attitude to Ireland. He began to write in Irish again, for the first time in twenty years. To find me in a school where nothing else was spoken seemed a good omen.

He had also re-discovered the GAA. The first person he met, when he arrived in Cork from Cobh, was a hotel porter who was having difficulty lifting the luggage, as four of his ribs were cracked and he was in some pain. He was a hurling goalkeeper and an opposing full forward had done the damage while bundling him into the net.

What impressed Liam, apart from the man's fortitude, was that he managed to clear the ball to safety and that he had no word of blame for the full forward, who was only doing his job, but was very angry with his own full back for not having stopped the forward as he was supposed to do.

As the following day was Sunday, Liam and the porter went off to a match in Thurles and Liam told me: "Then I really felt I was back in Ireland." I thought it better to explain that we played little or no hurling as the vast majority of students came from counties where football was the major game. Gaelic football had its points, he thought, but was infinitely inferior to hurling. But since he was told in Cork that hurling in Galway was in pretty bad shape, perhaps it was just as well to concentrate on football.

He was impressed by our ball-alleys and recalled how one could "buy" possession of an alley in Rockwell College with a slice of some sort of gur-cake, if the boy in possession happened to be a glutton. He made no mention at all of the only game he played competitively in Rockwell and Blackrock, but he may also have been told in Cork that rugby in Galway was in even worse shape than hurling.

But although I continued to practice right through my second last year in school, my enthusiasm for competitive games was already being diluted by other interests. In sport I found that "killing" a ball in the handball alley gave me a much more satisfying feeling than anything I experienced on the football field.

In fact I would probably have given up football completely, or else taken it up very seriously, had I been in a school where the numbers were greater and other forms of amusement scarcer than they were in Coláiste Einde. But I think I would have hated a school where supremacy in any sport was considered a matter of honour and of more importance than any other activity. In our case, the struggle to field a reasonably good team was challenge enough.

Two of our lay teachers devoted a lot of their spare time to developing our talents in other directions. Aodh Mac Dhúbháin, or Hudie as he was known to his students, taught us Irish, History and Geography and all sorts of general knowledge besides. As well as being a good teacher he was held in great affection by his pupils and when I began to travel around the country, and met past pupils of our school from previous years, I found that the first question they asked was invariably, "How is Hudie?" He was an actor and a translator of plays in Taibhdhearc na Gaillimhe and as if this was not enough, he also produced at least one play a year with the third or fourth year class in Coláiste Éinde.

Mícheál Mac Gabhna, unlike Hudie who was a native speaker from Trá Bháin in Connemara, was a Wicklowman and one of the first students to have come through the Preparatory system. He taught us English, Music, Drawing and Woodwork, gave tuition on the violin and piano and delighted in training choirs for competitions. He had a gift for composing and translating popular songs and for telling the tallest of stories with great conviction. During my last year he also helped us to organise a céilí band.

These two and an tAthair O Laoi helped to fill the gap in our information created by the absence of newspapers. Our hunger for news of domestic and foreign politics was such that any paper that came into our possession was passed from hand to hand until it fell apart.

Once, someone had a brainwave and suggested that the President order the weekly Irish language newspaper, *Inniu*. Dr O hEidhin listened to the prefect who was sent to bell the cat and said that he had a low opinion of the Irish used in the paper and that was the end of that.

When the Fianna Fáil Government was defeated in the 1947 election we were preparing for our Leaving Certificate and going mad for news. The radio was only available to us on major sporting occasions like the All-Ireland finals,

Máirtín Thornton's fights and de Valera's reply to Churchill. So we depended completely on these two teachers and an tAthair O Laoi to educate us in current affairs (a term not coined at the time) as well as in their chosen subjects.

Luckily for us they were all interested in politics and as our class was fairly hard-working, and hours of study were long, they were able to steal some time for our further enlightenment. As a result, I left school with a fairly detailed knowledge of such subjects as Saor Eire, the Republican Congress, the sacking of Frank Edwards, the jailing of Jim Larkin in the USA, the split in the Labour Party, the history of the split in Irish athletics and many more not easily available in books at the time. It was these informal chats in class and the weekly debate that first concentrated my mind on the GAA Ban on foreign games, which prohibited GAA members from playing or attending rugby, hockey, soccer or cricket.

The debates were held during second study on Saturday night, from 8.30 to 9.30, although they rarely ended on time. An tAthair O Laoi was usually on duty on Saturday nights and he presided over them, corrected false facts, became involved himself at times and got to know the most vociferous among us better than if he had been hearing our confessions for a month, non-stop. These debates were the high point of the week for those of us who had strong political or social opinions, for no holds were barred and there was complete freedom of expression; but one had to be careful, for wild arguments were subjected to fierce scrutiny and all shades of party politics were represented among us.

The motions for debate were a lot more ambitious than the tame, "Health is better than wealth" type of motion one encountered at feiseanna at the time. We got steamed up about the moral right of the IRA to make war on behalf of the Irish people, whether or not the Civil War was inevitable once the Treaty was signed (this one flushed out the pro- and anti-de Valera families, for most of us took our politics from home) and whether the GAA Ban was a help or a hindrance.

I have particularly clear memories of the latter debate. I was against the Ban for the simple, personal reason that I was interested in a variety of games, many of which I had not yet seen played, and had every intention of seeing them as soon as I could, without risk of demeaning my Irishness, or whatever it was the GAA was trying to protect for me. The interest was so great that the President came over from his office to find out why we were still in study instead of being in bed.

The debate continued in the dormitory and eventually an tAthair O Laoi had to light the lights again and blow the final whistle. He was in favour of the Ban but he held the ring fairly that night and the effect on me was the beginning of a critical attitude to the GAA as a national organisation.

An tAthair O Laoi, now a Canon and Parish Priest of Ennistymon, who has since written an interesting book, *Nora Barnacle*, and *The Annals of the GAA in Galway*, did a lot to broaden our vision. Although his temper was quick he always laced discipline with good humour and his cultivation of freedom of expression was appreciated by most of us, even at the time.

The high point of my involvement in football came when our team reached the final of the Connacht Colleges junior championship in 1947. We played St Jarlath's in the Sportsground, in Galway, and I still meet contemporaries who convince me that we might have won had not one of our best players, Deaglán O Braonáin from Meath, got acute appendicitis three weeks before the match. He tried to convince the authorities that he could play in goal without endangering his health but they knew very well that the plan was to switch him to his proper position as soon as the game started.

My own feeling is that we were half beaten before we started, as most of us realised that to have reached the final at all, in our peculiar circumstances, was in itself an achievement. The strength and tradition of our opponents ensured that we went out to give them a hard game. This we did, but they went out to add yet another trophy to the school's great collection. I have since recognised our symptoms in teams that reach the All-Ireland final, or semi-final, for the first time. To be there at all counts for too much and blunts further ambition.

I remember St Jarlath's as a well-trained and sporting team but as soon as the cup was presented I turned my mind to the match that was to follow: the West Board hurling final between Castlegar and Liam Mellows. As we returned to the dressing rooms, inside the Sportsground gate, the teams were going out on the field and the crowd that had watched our exertions in polite silence were beginning to buzz. Mellows and Cashel were always good value in those years.

I threw on my clothes and rushed out to see my first Galway senior hurling club game. As I turned the corner I met the teams coming back. Some players were spattered with blood, some were being restrained from further violence and everyone was in a state of high excitement. It seems that when the referee threw in the ball it was belted out over the sideline and the sixteen players in the centre of the field set about belting one another for reasons that remain obscure to this day. The referee ended the match that never really started.

This strange event made a much greater impression on me than the match I had played in and this may be the best comment on my own particular relationship with the GAA. However, many years later, it provided the germ of an idea out of which grew the novel *Lig Sinn i gCathú* (Lead us into Temptation).

Despite having had a very pleasant summer, or perhaps for that reason, I returned to complete my final year in a confused and discontented state of mind. Nothing about Coláiste Einde gave me any pleasure and I thought only of getting out. On the night of the All-Ireland final in the New York Polo Grounds, we were let off study to listen to Michael O Hehir's commentary. I have only a hazy recollection of it for I was taken ill suddenly, my temperature soared and I was removed to the Fever Hospital with suspected scarlet fever.

But it turned out to be an infection of the throat which cleared up far too quickly for my liking. The break with school routine, coming so soon after the long holidays, left me in an even greater state of dissatisfaction when I returned to the college.

Then one day, when rooting in an old outhouse, I found a coil of rope left over from the days of army occupation. I took it on impulse and hid it in my locker in the dormitory. The idea of getting out at night and walking the streets of Galway had been in my mind for some time. The difficulty lay in getting out without going downstairs while priests and staff were still on the prowl. Getting back in when they were safely in bed was not a problem.

Three of us made the first trip: tying the rope to the radiator under a window, shinning down and making a dash over the golf links wall, out on to the Rahoon Road and into Galway by side roads. An accomplice drew up the rope and replaced it in the hiding place. We had arranged dummy bodies in our beds and the others, who had designs on the rope themselves, promised to be orderly and not to attract attention while we were away.

We headed for an hotel on Eyre Square, where a lad who had once worked in Coláiste Einde was employed as a night porter. He put us in a small room near the kitchen and gave us bottles of stout and a plate of cold meat and bread. Some hours later we walked back to the college in great good humour, getting in through a ground floor window which we had unlatched during the day.

After two or three of these midnight flits a spirit of recklessness entered into us and the Donegal boys decided to go out to a dance. They were great ones for dancing and when they were not replaying football matches, they talked sentimentally about dances and the girls who were at that moment tossing and turning in their beds in the

Ursuline Convent in Sligo, in Coláiste Bhríde and in other centres of deprivation, until we were all in the condition for which the priest at the school retreat recommended a towel soaked in cold water and a decade of the rosary.

The group dressed up in their Sunday best and went to a dance in the Hangar Ballroom in Salthill. We were in a small dormitory and had anyone come in during their absence, the low level of breathing would have given the game away. As it was, one of them turned on his ankle on the way home and had to be carried back through the fields by the others.

The following day the senior prefect took me for a walk around the playing field and talked about the rope and the growth of recklessness. He was discreet and sensible and later took the rope and abandoned it where nobody was likely to find it. After that we all settled down to face the Leaving Certificate.

The incident is scarcely worth mentioning but for the fact that about eight years later, twelve students were expelled from Coláiste Einde, sent home in disgrace to their families, their careers ruined, for an escapade far less serious than ours.

I later discovered that these expulsions were used as an additional argument in favour of abolishing the Preparatory Colleges system, which happened in the early 1960s, when Dr Patrick Hillery was Minister for Education, as a result of pressure from the INTO, the authorities in the Teacher Training Colleges and some senior civil servants in the Department of Education. I was editor of the magazine *Comhar* at the time and wrote counselling caution and reform rather than abolition.

But I was told by leaders of the Irish language organisations that abolition would lead to higher standards of teaching as a result of a broader system of recruitment. They had also been assured that far from affecting the standard of Irish in the Training Colleges and in the primary schools adversely, the abolition would mean that the standard would shortly soar to new heights of fluency and perfection as a result of revolutionary linguistic innovations. Glowing in the warmth of these silken words they went happily away. In such a contest, duplicity will always knock the stuffing out of gullibility and subsequent events speak for themselves.

I merely wish to add this pebble of my own to the cairn that is rapidly forming over that particular grave. On the night that Seán O Ríordáin was dying in Sarsfield's Court Hospital in Cork, I was opening Irish Language Week in St Patrick's Training College, in Drumcondra. As I was not feeling particularly chirpy my speech was short and simple. Afterwards, the President thanked me graciously for coming and said, "I think *most* of the students understood you."

In a way it reminds me of the last game of football I ever played. It was in the first round of the Connacht Colleges senior championship against Roscommon CBS, in St Coman's Park, Roscommon. I was still in my uneasy mood, unfit and mentally unprepared and the longer the game lasted the longer and wider the park became. We were beaten and I had the stuffing knocked out of me by a malevolent corner forward who seemed to have at least twenty elbows, all mounted with cogs. At one point I tried to cripple him against the goalpost but missed, knocked over an umpire and got a few belts from some senior students of the school who were obviously too hairy for even this competition but were trying, with some success, to intimidate our goalkeeper.

After the match we were in Greally's Hotel, waiting for our meal, when the door of the dining room opened and the red-haired captain of the Roscommon team stuck in his head and uttered the unforgettable words, "Sorry, lads! No hard feelings!" and vanished before anyone could find something to bounce off his skull. But I had no hard feelings really. It was the end of something and we had lost but already something else far more important was filling my thoughts daily.

6

During the summer holidays my father was taken ill and I spent some weeks in charge of his classes. I liked the work and was glad of an opportunity to test myself in the real situation of the classroom. But I found the work exhausting and at the end of the first week I was fit for nothing but a very long sleep. The second week was worse. I lost my appetite and was in danger of losing my temper far too frequently, as well as suffering from splitting headaches.

My incipient hypochondria prompted me to go to Dr O'Brien for advice. The popular term that covered every illness from acne to depression, in those days, was "being run down", and I felt literally run down every evening at three, and sometimes hours before, and it took a lot of rest to charge my batteries for the following day's work.

The doctor took me very coolly and philosophically. He wondered aloud how someone who could even consider cycling half way across Ireland and back, to see a hurling match, could claim to be run down. When I pointed out to him that I could, at that very moment, scarcely cycle up the four hills to our house without dismounting four times for a rest, he began to explain different kinds of exhaustion to me. In different circumstances I might have found it very illuminating, for it ended as a lecture on D.H. Lawrence's short career as a teacher. What he was really telling me was that it took time to learn this seemingly simple trade properly, that there were no short cuts and that even at the best of times it was an exhausting occupation if pursued with due seriousness.

This left me feeling gutted. He did not even offer me one of his famous bottles of tonic, made up in front of your eyes in a disgustingly speckled enamel jug. Instead, he gave me *The White Peacock* and *Sea and Sardinia* and advised me to take as much rest as I felt was necessary. But his explanation (since confirmed for me many times by young teachers) was no consolation at all and I felt very sorry for myself.

As it was taken for granted by my parents that I would go to the training college, all being well, and as I was the eldest of four and expected to give good example, I decided to bottle up my misgivings and gradually day-dreamed into a state of depression, particularly after I returned to Coláiste Einde.

I would certainly be a bad teacher and would un-doubtedly end up in one of those two-teacher schools in Leitrim, Laois or Monaghan that had already entered into the folklore of Coláiste Einde. Some of the most notorious past pupils were languishing in various inaccessible moun-tainy regions of Ireland, avoiding the Marlborough Street posse.

There I would sit in bad digs, drinking whiskey and poitín with the alcoholic curate, bank manager and agri-cultural instructor, fighting with the manager of the school, running the gauntlet of inspection, harassed by parents whose children were running wild and illiterate, with only my faithful female assistant to succour and pro-tect me. Then, one bleak March morning, as I was curing myself from the bottle I kept hidden in the turf-shed, my assistant would embrace me tearfully with the dread news, "Jesus, Breandán, I'm nearly two weeks overdue and me as regular as a clock! What are you going to do about it?" After that there was only the Furry Glen Publishing com-pany and the long road, or the Holyhead boat and the rough lie-down in Camden Town.

Every morning in the chapel I added another scene to

my sad scenario. The chapel was the best place for day-dreaming for, unlike the classroom or the study hall, a blank expression could be attributed to an excess of piety bordering on ecstasy. The American novelist, John Updike, has said that he finds the atmosphere at Sunday morning service conducive to working out his plots and developing his characters. Be that as it may, I worked out the solution to my non-fictional problem during mass one morning.

I would have to win a scholarship to the university as Declan Brennan (as Deaglán was now known in the reality of life without the walls) had done the previous year and who was now enjoying life in UCG and the fleshpots of Galway to boot. The thought had previously crossed my mind but as I had never exerted myself in the subjects that did not come easily to me, I was overwhelmed by the thought of the leeway that had to be made up. This particular morning it seemed that it might be possible to do that in a little over two terms.

I began to work hard for the first time in my life and soon I was waking myself an hour before the seven o'clock bell to brush up my Latin and the detested Maths, Chemistry and Physics. My teachers encouraged me and the last two terms passed so quickly that few clear memories of anything but learning remain. The Leaving Certificate and the Matriculation (which I sat in order to enter for yet another university scholarship) dominated everything else, and I felt neither joy nor sorrow as I walked towards the docks for the last time as a schoolboy.

At home I was outwardly non-committal but confident that I would take one of the three classes of scholarship available and swim past the net of primary teaching. I controlled my sense of impending elation but was cheerful enough to return to the scene of my marked lack of success in St Coman's Park, Roscommon.

The Connacht Final, between Mayo and Galway, in 1948, was a tremendous game by all accounts and ended in a draw. The replay was fixed for the first Sunday in August, also in Roscommon, and I made up my mind to go after meeting Bartley Gill in Kilronan late on Friday evening. He had a boat called the "Alice Webster" and he mentioned that he was going to Leitir Meallàin the following morning to collect lobsters. I decided there and then to take up my bike and travel.

I must really have been feeling well for there was a regular sailing to and from Galway that Saturday and one look at the map will show that travelling from Aran to Roscommon, via Leitir Meallàin, is rather like going from Dublin to Mullingar through Athlone. My father had gone to Clare and I was on the road on my own for the first time. My spirits were still high as we left Kilronan on one of those summer mornings when the bay shone like silver before gradually turning various shades of blue. Bartley Gill was one of a clan that could easily be traced to one Hugh Gill, a boatbuilder, who came from Westport and settled in Kilronan and whose descendants were as prolific as he was.

I seem to have spent a great deal of my youth in the company of the old and elderly and although I was talkative from an early age, I was also a good listener. Bartley Gill was a gruff and kindly man who had spent more of his life on sea than on land and that morning he passed the time between Kilronan and Leitir Meallàin by naming the different breakers along the coast and pointing out different markings that fishermen used in the days before more sophisticated methods of fishing.

Bartley Gill, although he was bilingual, always spoke Irish to me. Dr O'Brien, who was younger than him, never spoke Irish to me for the simple reason that he spoke it like a learner and was only at home in the English language. Like the sea that sparkles at its feet, the two languages ebbed and flowed in Kilronan for many years. For me it is always Kilronan and not Cill Rónáin for some inexplicable reason.

Shortly after being put ashore in Leitir Meallàin my spirits began to sink and my flesh weakened perceptibly. I was bored on my own and by the time I arrived in Casla the tar was hissing under my tyres from the heat. When I reached Baile na hAbhann I threw in the towel, let the wind out of one of my tyres, hid my repair kit and hitched a lift from a jolly lorry driver from Tuam who threw the bike on top of his load of turf and shortened the road to Galway with a series of parables which proved conclusively that Galway would beat Mayo in the replay.

The following morning, having completely forgotten to get a pump to inflate my tyre, I went happily to Roscommon on a crowded train from Galway. My cycling days were coming to an end.

The game was worth coming a long way to see. Jack Mahon, who has written extensively on Gaelic games, and has seen many more Connacht finals than I have, rates it among the best he has seen. For teamwork, for brilliant individual performances and for sustained, hard competitiveness up to the last kick, I must rate it the best Connacht final I have seen and one of the best provincial finals played before the changes in the rules and the introduction of the seventy minute game.

Galway had players like Joe Duggan, Seán Thornton and Jarlath Canavan who had already given of their best and were soon to retire. They also had Seán Purcell, Frank Stockwell and Jack Mangan, just out of minor and school-boy football, who were to help to bring an All-Ireland to the county eight years later.

Mayo had already almost fashioned that team of stars — the greatest to represent the county in a hundred years — that went on to contest that year's All-Ireland unsuccessfully against Cavan and then won two in a row, against Louth and Meath, in 1950 and 1951.

The game went to extra time and was won by Seán Mulderrig for Mayo with a truly brilliant goal. On the way home on the train it was agreed, in my carriage at least, that while Pádraig Carney was the top scorer for Mayo and Seán Purcell the outstanding mid-fielder of the four, the man of the match was Tom Sullivan of Uachtar Ard. Tom was a younger brother of Dinny, star left corner back on the Galway team of 1938. Tom Sullivan was one of the most graceful fielders and kickers of a ball that I have ever seen. When I think of great footballers who never won an All-Ireland medal I immediately think of Tom Sullivan. His taking of a penalty that day, after Stockwell was taken down in the square, would serve as an example for any footballer, amateur or professional. He hit it high into the angle of crossbar and goalpost after taking no more than three steps.

There was no dishonour in this defeat and I noticed that day, as I have often noticed since, that once the provincial battle is over in Connacht — and battle is not too strong a word to use to describe some of the games I have seen — the ranks are quickly closed and everyone supports the champions as if they were his own team. I think this trait, which one finds elsewhere of course, is more pronounced in Connacht. It may be somewhat fanciful to see it as part of Cromwell's legacy but I saw this strange brotherhood in action in a different way in London dance halls when shouts of "Roscommon", "Mayo", or "Galway" would go up as reinforcements were sought to make common cause against the alien hordes from across the Shannon. I also noticed that everyone made common cause when the enemy was the Dublin Jackeen, who, despite this united front of knuckles and boots, was always able to give as good as he got.

A lot of great minors came of age that day in Roscommon: Seán Purcell, Pádraig Carney, Frank Stockwell, Peter Solan, Jack Mangan, Seán Mulderrig, Billy Kenny, Pat McAndrew. . . . It may prove a point I have frequently heard that minors are held back too long at the present time, and that the under-21 competition is partly responsible. Of course, many good minors vanish without trace and it often struck me that one of the saddest things you can hear said of a hurler or a footballer is, "He was a great minor". Without the all-important "also" it is a very short story of much promise not fulfilled.

Shortly after arriving back in Aran, and even before my

marks arrived, I was informed that I had won a scholarship worth £150 a year to UCG and could study any subject I wished. I had escaped the net. The fact that I had not the remotest notion what I wanted to do in the university, much less what I wished to do later, bothered me not in the slightest. I was free and almost financially independent and that was more than I could clearly comprehend and something I was neither trained nor mentally prepared for.

Later, it could be truly said of my achievement that, like the man who was a great minor, nothing in my academic life became me like my Leaving Cert.

In these days of breakneck inflation it may seem ridiculous to find me talking of partial independence on £150 a year. To put that sum in perspective, let me point out that the annual fee for Arts (which was the faculty my inclinations chose) was £20. My first digs cost £2.00 a week, full board, and my last — in a hotel — three pounds and ten shillings.

In those days a pint of stout cost 10d. and a bottle 7d. When I stupidly began to smoke, a packet of twenty cigarettes cost a shilling and eight pence. Admission prices to cinemas and most dances were halved for students. I do not remember ever having to part with money at the Sportsground gate. I was always a good walker and climber and chose to come over the wall on the Bohermore, or cemetery, side of the ground. The town was also full of free, or almost free, entertainment.

At an early stage in my career the university began to lose to the town and by the time I reached the end of my three idyllic years the university could not even remain in contention. In his book, *An Irish Journey*, Seán O Faoláin writes that "no man who wants his daughter to learn the truth about life could do better than send her for six months to Galway." He imagines her returning and asking him if all she has heard there is the truth and he will reply, "Of course it is not the truth. But it *is* life." O Faoláin concludes that "Galway is and lives a folk-tale."

Why daughters should be singled out for this desirable

course of education in life is not clear, but allowing for a modicum of the Blarney one finds when travel writers try to pin down an atmosphere they find appealing but cannot accurately analyse, O Faoláin comes as close as anyone I have read to isolating a major part of the charm of Galway.

It is something more than charm. There is an absence of fanaticism in the air that is a blessing in a country plagued by preachers and cursed with concrete-bedded stances for and against theories. Not wishing to shipwreck this paragraph on a reef of generalisations let me just say that at a time when tolerance was at a premium in this island there was a warm bed of it in Galway, even if one had to enter it through a window that was dressed in conventional artifice.

My academic career could be written on the back of a large stamp. I scraped through first year with the two honours necessary to hold my scholarship. Irish I abandoned out of sheer boredom, coupled with horror at the prospect of having to study Old Irish. So I stayed with English and History, taking Philosophy as a third subject, partly out of interest in the discipline and partly out of curiosity to examine Professor Feidhlim O Briain at close quarters. I had begun to read *The Irish Times* and Dr O Briain was stuck into Dr Sheehy Skeffington and others in a long disputation on the Liberal Ethic and later on the Dr Noel Browne affair.

Professor O Briain was a mild-looking Franciscan friar but his philosophy was several leagues to the right of Pope Pius XII. But unlike the other lecturers I encountered, the intensity of his views forced anyone who took his subjects seriously to think for himself — even though he might also have to keep those thoughts severely to himself.

The English course was heavily ballasted with Old English and the novel seemed to end with Thomas Hardy, which even in the early fifties was a somewhat high cut. Once, in an unthinking moment and before I learned to keep my own thoughts on certain subjects to myself, I mentioned a story by Ernest Hemingway, whom I had just discovered, and it was pointed out to me that if I wanted journalism I had a wide choice of newspapers in Holland's Newsagent's every morning. The story was "Fifty Grand" and I have always regarded it as the finest short story — bar none — with a sports theme.

But having come to university merely to avoid having to go elsewhere, I did not arrive with great expectations. Nevertheless, it came as something of a shock to find the English course so dull and the History lectures so tedious, for the quality of teaching in Coláiste Einde had prepared me for something more exciting.

If a little boredom was the price I had to pay for being free to do as I wished outside the lecture rooms, I was willing to pay it. In my secret heart I had decided to do everything that was necessary to prolong the life of my scholarship, read everything that interested me, enjoy the life of Galway and see what happened afterwards. But some secrets are best shared and into town blew Liam and based himself in the Great Southern Hotel while trying to finish his novel, *Insurrection*. It was giving him a lot of trouble and his mood was a daily indication of how the work was proceeding.

John Moynihan, who was hall porter in the Southern for many years, was able to read Liam's moods accurately and mark my cards accordingly. I then knew when to call and when to leave him to wrestle with his problem. We had some good days and even better nights during his three month stay in Galway, but whatever romantic illusions I may have had about a writer's life were soon demolished by the sight of Liam after an unsuccessful day at the typewriter in the solitude of a hotel-room.

We talked of life in the university and we both agreed that as far as lecturing was concerned I would be better off listening to Dr O'Brien discussing Melville, Lawrence or the Dublin of *Ulysses*. However, this was an opportunity to read widely and well and being an early bird himself, he advised me to spend as much of the early part of the day as possible in the library. To prime my pump, as it were, he took me to Kenny's Bookshop and bought me a dozen of the Everyman Library translations of the great Russian writers. Holding on to my scholarship was very important. He had been about to lose his, thirty five years previously in UCD, for non-attendance at lectures, and that was one of the reasons he joined the British Army, under the name Bill Ganly, in 1915. By enlisting he saved the scholarship, although he never used it afterwards.

When he was in one of his optimistic moods, Liam would convince me that his friend Monsignor Pádraig de Brún would set all UCG's problems and shortcomings to rights as soon as he settled into the presidency. Later it occurred to me that Liam saw more of Pádraig de Brún during his three months in Galway than my contemporaries did in the course of three years. He was always remote from the student body and we felt that he was never completely at ease in his position.

I had good reason to be grateful to him when I was reported to the College authorities for staying in a licensed premises (which was a breach of College rules, although I had my parents' permission to stay in the Castle Hotel) and for not attending mass. My coarser friends maintained that the girls from the UCG division of the Legion of Mary, who had been keeping an eye on my Sunday morning movements, were merely suffering from a basic deprivation, but I had to go to the President's office.

He was kind and gentle and gave me good advice, ending with the words, "Go away now and be careful, and remember that I am not the highest ecclesiastic authority in this city." The Dean of Residence, who kept an eye on our moral welfare, was also secretary to Bishop Browne, and as I noted in the case of Coláiste Éinde, Bishop Browne did not approve of institutions over which he did not have total control.

Organised social activities in College were of little interest to me. I never attended a dance, preferring to go to the halls where céilithe were held which were wilder and much more interesting and not frequented by many of the students. For a short time I was involved with An Cumann Eigse agus Seanachais but withdrew when we were refused permission to have Máirtín O Cadhain as a speaker during the annual Irish Week. None of us had ever seen or heard him but most of us were reading *Cré na Cille* which *The Irish Press* was serialising at the time. We were told that he was not considered a suitable person to address us and that was the end of that.

I later found out that it was Professor Liam O Buachalla, still smarting from his defeat in the election for the Presidency of the Gaelic League some years previously by Seán Og O Tuama (who was locked up in the internment camp in the Curragh with Máirtín O Cadhain and others at the time), who decided to put his foot down. In Galway, very little was secret for long if you kept your ear to the right keyhole. For my part, I think I welcomed a fairly dramatic excuse to get off the only committee I sat on while a student.

Máirtín, when he heard of the affair, chose to blame Monsignor de Brún, saying that the captain is responsible for the running of the ship, even if he is sleeping when a mistake is made. But the matter was a little more complicated than that. It seems that someone had told Máirtín that Monsignor de Brún was heard to pass a disparaging remark about *Cré na Cille* to a companion on a Dublin bus. Wonderful, indeed, are the workings of the convoluted Celtic mind!

That was the extent of my involvement in organised activities, but small as it was it became very important later when I was desperately looking for a job and the experience had to be suitably extended and exaggerated. The glimpse it afforded of what is now known to me as "the spleen-divided Gael" was useful in later life also.

My experience of life in Galway in the early fifties could easily run away with this book, for I was in an ideal situation to spend long hours and days moving through it like a fish swimming in a large tank. The temptation to digress is strong but I intend to resist it as strongly as I can and confine myself to the central theme.

For one thing, all the principal field sports were played in the city and it was also a strong centre of rowing. This afforded me my first opportunity of seeing games I had been reading about ever since I inherited Roger Hammond's collection of books and comics.

Two visits to Terryland Park gave me my fill of soccer. Bad gaelic football and bad rugby football can bore me to the point when I say to myself, "Why don't these fellows find themselves a different game to play?"; bad soccer always forces me to ask myself, "Why don't these people give up?" This may be because the gap between good and bad is so wide in the case of the world's most popular ball game. Of course, these conclusions only arise when I am asked to pay to watch these activities. What consenting adults do to amuse themselves is an entirely different matter.

Apart from a period in Dublin, when my room-mate Jack Ryan was a delegate to the League of Ireland, and took me to matches when Shamrock Rovers and Waterford were playing, I never developed an interest in domestic soccer and what interest I had was killed stone dead by the advent of television.

I went to hockey matches. Played by girls I found the sport entertaining and pleasantly titillating, as well as being more graceful than what little camogie I had seen. Hockey played by men, I am afraid, suffered badly in the obvious comparison with hurling. It looked effeminate and somehow theatrical. To my eye, the difference is comparable to that between a display of Morris dancing in Covent Garden Market, under the auspices of the cultural department of the Greater London Council, and a Clare set danced on the flagged floor of a pub by a group from Mullagh or Quilty; and that, in case you do not know, is to set dancing what Cork or Kilkenny are to hurling.

Cricket I saw played in the Old Grammar School pitch but it left me stone cold, although I found John Arlott's radio commentaries relaxing and full of magic which I did not fully understand. Not until one of my sons sat me down in front of the television set and explained the coarser and finer points of the game to me, did I become fascinated by it. Its roots — its *dúchas* — were first revealed to me one day in Richmond, Surrey, as I sat and watched a match played on the village green between two teams of very aggressive young boys.

Indeed, did not Michael Cusack himself write that, "it is a splendid game when well played" and again, "there is no better game for lads to play". He merely criticised the cricket authorities at home for not cultivating willow and making bats instead of importing bats made of English willow. One wonders what he would have to say today about the GAA's neglect of the ash.

Not unlike Cusack, in his pre-1884 years, I was experiencing all the available sports and observing those who played and followed them. Cusack wrote: "I was in and through all these camps. I admired them greatly; because of their splendid, sleepless and persistent intolerance. My admiration will not surprise anyone when I avow that I have never met a man more intolerant than myself."

Mention of intolerance brings me directly to the Ban and the game of rugby: a game that Cusack also played with some distinction. The eventual demise of the Ban in 1971, and the campaigns for and against it which preceded that important event in the history of the GAA, I propose to deal with at a later stage, when looking at the general area of politics and the GAA in the Northern state. At this stage I was beginning to see for myself what was happening in various areas of Irish life. The Ban as a subject for debate in school was remote; the Ban as I saw it operated in Galway and as it directly affected my friends was now a daily fact of life and a rather confusing and uncomfortable one.

It was through rugby and not through soccer that I became aware of that reality. There is a long tradition of rugby in Galway: the first Connacht Cup was won by Galway Town in 1896 and the following year it was won by Queen's College, as UCG was then known. The game remained strong in the university and UCG won the Cup six times, between 1939 and 1946, one of their best forwards during this period being Donough O'Malley, later Minister for Education, who also played for Connacht.

The first UCG player to be capped for Ireland was Dick Roche, from Woodford, a past pupil of Garbally College, Ballinasloe, as were internationals Mick Molloy, Ray and Phelim McLaughlin and Ciarán Fitzgerald. Hurling and rugby were the principal games played in Garbally, and like Mount St Joseph's Abbey in Roscrea, where the situation was the same, the school also specialised in athletics. But because Garbally competed in the Connacht Colleges rugby competition (against Sligo and Galway Grammar schools and Collegians of Galway City) their hurlers could not compete in the GAA colleges competition. Joe Salmon, one of the finest hurlers of his generation, played rugby for Garbally and for Connacht schools before he became a county hurler.

To complicate matters further, and to add to my own confusion as I surveyed the scene, Collegians were really St Joseph's College, Nun's Island, (known in Galway as "The Bish") under a pseudonym which was recommended by the Patrician Brothers to circumvent the Ban. Theoretically at least, the boys who played rugby for Collegians were not supposed to play gaelic football or hurling for "The Bish". Tony O'Sullivan, who played rugby with distinction for Ireland on fifteen occasions before being dropped for no good reason that anyone outside of the inner masonry of the IRFU could see, was the best-known player to come through that particular shortcut through the Ban.

Even in those days, rugby in Galway City, and to a greater extent in Limerick, was played by the same classes who played gaelic football, hurling and soccer. They did not necessarily play on the same teams, some clubs being choosier than others in matters of recruitment, but they were involved in the same competitions. It was played by much smaller numbers, of course, and was distinguished from other popular sports by the fact that it was played by Protestants and by the sons of small-town businessmen who had been sent to the rugby-playing academies of Blackrock, Castleknock and Clongowes Wood, to ensure that they were kept a cut above the buttermilk that surrounded them at home and to make useful business connections.

When I was living in Lower Abbeygate Street, I made the acquaintance of some gentlemen of no property or worries who spent dry days polishing the walls of the Four Corners and other vantage points, like the Lazy Wall, with their arses and elbows, and watching the world pass by. These men followed Rovers soccer team, Rovers junior rugby team, Liam Mellows hurling team, and they were careful never to miss any of the matches between Castlegar and Turloughmore, played in the Sportsground — for aesthetic reasons which will be made clear later.

I went over the wall in their company many times and can vouch for the fact that gaelic football was more of a foreign game to them than any of the ones they followed.

Like Eamon de Valera, I came to the conclusion that hurling and rugby football were particularly suited to the Irish temperament. The standard of rugby in Connacht at the time was not particularly high but I had the good fortune to see Jack Kyle play for Ulster in the Sportsground, and little as I knew about the niceties of the game, I would have known, had I not already been fully aware, that this was a player of genius. For one thing, his togs were as clean at half-time as they were when the game started, in heavy rain, and the only reason they were muddy at the game's end was that he had slid over for a spectacular try.

I voiced my opinion to Liam, which was really preaching to the long-converted. He told me that the famous Ryan brothers, Jack and Mick, whom he had seen in Rockwell and who had played for Ireland between 1897 and 1904, had also played gaelic football for Tipperary when the Ban on foreign games was lifted between 1895 and 1902.

Eamon de Valera, who was once tossed across a table in Rockwell by Mick Ryan as Ryan demonstrated the "bit of a fwuip" he had used to throw an English player into the touchline seats in Lansdowne Road a few days previously, would have been well advised to have kept his views on hurling and rugby inside his family circle too. Instead he once made them public on what he thought was a private occasion. I referred to this instance in a column I once wrote on sporting matters and got the following letter from a reader who was present on the occasion:

It was the annual dinner of Blackrock College Old Boys, and was held in Shannon Airport Restaurant. Dev, whose sight had failed, had established a splendid rapport with those in his immediate vicinity and there was a very warm and cheerful atmosphere. Amongst those at Dev's table was the *Irish Times* reporter at Shannon. *Dev did not know this.*

In the usual glowing interval after the speeches and before "break-up" the talk revolved around the fact that Rockwell was one of the few schools that played both hurling and rugby, and it was during this chat that Dev remarked that "he believed that those were the games best suited to the Irish temperament" (And who will contradict that?)

There can be no doubt but that this remark was made by Dev, in a tone that suggested that it was his considered opinion, as the news of the remark flashed around the other tables, and was the prime topic of conversation for some minutes.

It happened that this was one of the periods when the Ban controversy was on the boil, and anyone voicing anti-Ban sentiments was regarded as a very poor Irishman indeed.

You can imagine the shock that Dev got next morning, to find what he thought was his private opinion and private remarks trumpeted in the papers. Efforts to play it down were more or less successful, but what surprised many was the fact that no attack came from the ranks of the GAA. Obviously because of his high standing. Dev was Taoiseach at the time, and he feared that the Party would suffer by reason of his remarks.

That gives a better idea of what feelings were like at the time than anything that happened in Galway in my days as a student, for the atmosphere there was not as poisonous in this matter as it was in other places. For the hurling men, outside the city, the Ban meant little more than a word they heard used by people who attacked the GAA.

But there was a Vigilance Committee appointed by the County Board to keep attendances and players at foreign games under observation and report sightings of GAA members to the County Board who then sat in judgement on them. The following reminscence of the Ban in its hey-day appeared in the Galway *GAA Annual* for 1980 and it gives the flavour of the period perfectly:

The curate and I drove twenty miles to the Sports-ground to see the County Hurling final. We were early and bought the Sunday papers to while away the time. We were surprised to find the main gate wide open, and no official in sight to take up the shilling. A cheer from the few spectators alerted us to the fact that a football game was in progress. We sat by the wayside reading our newspapers. After an interval the spectators began to move towards the exit. Because I had a shilling in my pocket and on my conscience, I joined the crowd.

The main gate was now closed, but not for long. A crash of missiles on the zinc warned of an ugly situation outside. The gates gave way before a heaving mass of hurling supporters. To avoid the mob I stepped aside, but right into the path of the County Chairman, who collared me. "Were you at the rugby match?" he demanded. That was the first I knew of a rugby match. "No I wasn't," I replied. Because of the confusion he was forced to unhand me.

Two days later I had a letter from him, inviting me to a County Board meeting in the Royal Hotel to explain my presence at a rugby match. I replied by return refusing his invitation, and letting him know that I did not wish to be considered in future for the senior hurling team.

That was a fairly usual occurrence, as the GAA had no ground of its own in Galway City at the time and had to share the Sportsground with other organisations. The Vigilance Committee spent a lot of time there trying to spot their straying sheep among the graceless goats. A peak cap pulled down over the eyes, a scarf worn high across the face, the loan of a friend's gaberdine or crombie overcoat, were some of the recommended disguises of the period for those who chose to run the gauntlet.

There were also fringe lunacies to be observed. Once, during a meeting of the County Board, in the Royal Hotel, it was discovered that an important hurling match would have to be played in the Sportsground, after a rugby match, as that fixture was already booked for three o'clock. The ground was soft and it was desirable that the hurlers play before it was churned up by the scrums. A well-informed delegate said that as the rugby people were having a meeting in the hotel at the time they might, if requested, agree to switch the fixture and come to an agreement about starting times.

That was accepted as a good idea but it created procedural difficulties. It would be illegal for a GAA spokesman to attend a rugby meeting, and it would be improper, if not also illegal, to admit a rugby spokesman to a GAA meeting. After long discussion it was decided, through the good offices of the hotel receptionist, to set up an informal get-together in yet another room in the hotel. This was done and the matter was resolved in a matter of minutes.

It is important that younger readers understand that

these were times of great paternalism. Various organisations and institutions tried to keep their members on the straight and narrow path of virtue, from conception to resurrection. To do this it was also necessary to protect them from vice. My own pursuit by the Legion of Mary was an example of a vigilance committee seeking non-attenders at a religious arena.

The censorship boards that read books and viewed films were also set up to shield our virtue from evil and those who criticised their activities too severely often found themselves branded as agents of evil — much in the same way as those who protest too loudly against the operation of Section 31 of the Broadcasting Act, in present-day Ireland, may find themselves branded as agents of subversion.

My first brush with the censorship of books and periodicals was a lot funnier than my brush with those who wished me to go to mass for the good of my soul — which merely succeeded in making me pretend to go, for the good of my scholarship and a quiet life. Someone in our group discovered that one of the biggest bookshops in London sent books out on approbation and we agreed that the matter called for exploitation. We organised two or three accommodation addresses and some false names and the books began to flow. When the firm wrote, demanding the books or their value, the letters were returned marked, "Gone to USA" or, "Not known at this address".

During this short, but rewarding, foray into the world of commerce and importation, the list from one of our addresses included *The Good Soldier Sveik* (which I had recently read about) and *The Encyclopaedia of Sex* (which was the price demanded by our contact in the accommodation address). When the parcel arrived my book was missing and an enclosed note informed me that it was banned by the Censorship Board. I was as angry as if I had intended to pay for it, but my anger disappeared when I saw that the sex book had in fact come through. It was a very plain-looking book, was written by a gentleman called Anthony Havil, B.A. and must have been mistaken by the customs men as a work of some academic merit. It circulated widely in the Shantalla area of the town until a landlady who, unlike its other readers, had the means of putting its theories to the test, placed it under her pillow for keeps.

The GAA Ban did not affect me directly, as I was now a mere spectator and could view as I pleased, but it did affect some of my friends. My classmate, Seán McKeever, took up rugby in UCG and finding it more to his taste than gaelic football he decided to concentrate all his energies on it. Declan Brennan, who won an All-Ireland junior title with Meath and also played with them in the senior final against Cavan in 1952, decided to try his luck with gaelic and rugby. His luck lasted through his studies in Galway but in 1953 he was reported for playing rugby with Drogheda Town, where he was then teaching, and suspended for six months. However, to ensure that his prospects as a county player were truly blighted he was not reinstated for two years. Of all my friends, he was, and still remains, the most involved and dedicated member of the GAA.

Gaelic football and hurling were very strong in UCG during that period. The hurling team had the services of Joe Salmon and Miko McInerney, who captained the county team during his student years. The footballers had Billy Kenny, Peter Solan and Mick O'Malley of Mayo, Christy Garvey of Roscommon (who must hold some sort of record for Sigerson Cup appearances) and Seán Purcell, after he qualified as a national teacher.

My only memory of the Ban as a matter of public contention concerns a debate on the issue in the Literary and Debating Society. Temperatures rose briefly when the two principal speakers against the Ban, Seán McKeever and Dónal O Súileabháin from Corca Dhuibhne (who was captain of the rugby team) began their speeches in Irish. Some of the pro-Ban faction, who were well represented in the hall, took this to be an oblique comment on the lip service to the language of which the GAA was often accused.

A variation on that theme had been current in Galway since the 1951 General Election campaign when, it was said, Seán MacBride spoke in Eyre Square and paid *lisp* service to the language. It was not a terribly funny pun but people were sensitive because of it. But the row really started when someone suggested that, as the Ban represented an extreme form of nationalism, it was only right and proper that the debate be conducted completely in Irish. I was much amused by the animosity towards Irish shown by some of the most vehement supporters of the Ban when they lost their tempers and the thin skin of pretence came off — like so many tomatoes dipped in boiling water.

But it was also in Galway that the following incident occurred, during the last years of the Ban. The county selectors were beginning to build the team that eventually won three All-Irelands in a row between 1964 and 1966. A promising player who was a student in UCG came to their notice and they tried him successfully in a challenge match. He was placed on the panel and his friends advised him to end his connection with the UCG junior rugby team with which he had been involved with distinction: he had helped the team to reach the final of the Connacht Cup, a fact not known to the county selectors.

He approached the rugby team and they looked at him with great disfavour. Was he really going to desert them at the last ditch? What about the honour of UCG? He began to relent, and was convinced when a bright spark suggested that he stay out of the team photograph which would appear in the *Connacht Tribune*. His name in the match report could be explained as an error by an incompetent reporter provided his picture did not appear. He was convinced.

But Jimmy Walshe, who was then a photographer with the *Tribune* and a rugby player himself, had an eye like a hawk and a nose for a mystery. He noticed that there were only fourteen players in the group and spotting the shy one, waited for the right moment in the game to get a good head and shoulders. And that was why the winning UCG team appeared the following week, complete with the missing one's inset.

Delicate GAA approaches were met with equally delicate reassurances that this was the last hurrah and that the round ball would now rule without a rival. All was soon forgiven and forgotten as he helped the county team go from strength to strength.

Then one Sunday morning, some years after RTE had brought sex and other foreign games to the most remote homes in Ireland, our hero was travelling to a match with some team-mates and the most venerable GAA personage in the county. The venerable one had obviously sinned against the spirit, if not the letter, of the sacred rule the previous day, which happened to have been the day of an international rugby match, for he asked, "Tell me, lads, what in the name of God is this thing they call 'the loose head'?"

After the predictable jeering and ribbing had died down, our hero called out from the back seat, "Surely you know that! Don't you remember that picture of me in the *Connacht Tribune*?"

7

Early in the summer of 1950 I was mooning about the house, complaining of boredom, when my mother suggested, out of a clear sky, that it might be good for me to go to Rome for a Holy Year pilgrimage. Not having much interest in pilgrimages, but being sorely tempted by the money she offered to get me to Rome and back, I decided to hit the road and see what happened.

London seemed the ideal place from which to start, and the road to London began in Galway railway station. Galway station was the busiest place in the town every afternoon during those years, as hundreds of men and women -- most of them pathetically young -- took the boat-train to Dún Laoire, Holyhead and the cities beyond. For them the journey was a necessity, but for me it was the beginning of the greatest adventure of my life, so far.

Before the train reached Athlone I fell in with a group of young men who were speaking Irish in the bar. They were from Connemara, some returning to London, others making the trip for the first time. The next best thing to meeting someone from the island was to meet a Connemara-man, no matter where you were. At Euston the group split up, with promises to meet in a pub in Hammersmith on the following Friday night.

I went with three of them to a digs near the Elephant and Castle which had been recommended by someone who was either a bad judge of digs or an enemy in disguise. It was a dreadful place and reminded me immediately of a contemporary cartoon in *Dublin Opinion* which was a comment on a speech made by Eamon de Valera, at a St Patrick's Day dinner in Birmingham, attacking the terrible conditions in some of the lodging houses where Irish emigrants lived. He had heard of cases where the beds were in constant use, by day and by night. The cartoon showed about eight men squashed in a bed with Dev standing beside it, undressing. The caption read, "Shove over, lads! Dev's home off the night-shift."

Even the cold kip in wartime Dublin was a home from home in comparison with this airless, stinking doss-house which was run by a tiny Englishwoman with dyed hair and an aggressive Welshman with tattooed arms, whom I took to be her husband. He did nothing but issue instructions, collect the money a week in advance and move between the house, the pub and the illegal bookies' runners. But she was a war widow and he was living off her, a situation known in the rough jargon of the day as "cock-lodging". He was a born thug and looked it, but as if that were not enough he kept reminding anyone who complained about the least thing that he had been a champion boxer in the navy.

My companions went to work on the site of the Festival of Britain and offered to get me started there whenever I wished. But my mother's money was burning a hole in my pocket and there was the London I had read so much about in the books of Captain Marryat and others to explore. So I spent my first week seeing the sights by day, and my nights doing the rounds of the Irish pubs and dance halls. My friends thought I had the life of Riley and encouraged me to make the most of it: finding a job was easy when the time came. The Welshman had other ideas.

He came in with the paper late one morning, when the house was supposed to be empty, to find me drinking tea in the kitchen and chatting to his meal-ticket who was sitting in her dressing-gown, smoking. I was too green to know that cock-lodgers had little security of tenure, that supply far exceeded demand, and that Irishmen were in greater demand than any other nationality by landladies who ran lodging-houses for the Irish. Apart from the fact that they were better at keeping their own in line, by fair means or foul, there were ways of getting them to live up to their religious beliefs and marry — even when they already had a wife at home.

All this I learned later. At that moment all I got was my walking-papers, delivered with a remark that this was not "an 'ostel for bleedin' professors". I left with the relief of the indolent person, forced into action by circumstances not of his own making.

But I did loathe the Welshman and hoped never to cross his path again. Five years later, while going home for Christmas on the Galway train, I met one of my companions from that summer who wanted to know the circumstances of my sudden departure from the digs. He himself had left shortly afterwards but one of his friends stayed on, for some inexplicable reason. It was from him he learned of the Welshman's literal downfall.

It was connected with that year's football championship, much as that fact might have puzzled the Welshman. 1950 was Mayo's year of football glory and when the Irish in Britain were not discussing the job, or the three Rs (the Rake of beer, the Rear-Up and the Ride) they talked incessantly about the matches back home. As I remember it now, Kerry were supposed to meet Mayo in the final, and bets were being laid even before either team had won the provincial final. It was my first experience of this extended GAA family across the sea.

In August, Mayo beat Armagh easily, in the semi-final, and late that night, when rumour was confirmed by one of the Irish newspaper offices in Fleet Street (in those days it was not possible to receive Radio Eireann in London), some Mayo lodgers in our old digs smuggled a few friends, a lot of booze and a mouth organ, into their room, locked the door and had a party.

The Welshman was roused from his luxurious bed by the

strains of that great Western anthem, "The Boys from the County Mayo", accompanied by shouts of "Up Mayo" and "We never died a Winter yet", exactly as if they were on the train home from Croke Park. Failing to persuade them to open up and have manners beaten into them, the Welshman resorted to abuse and the phrase "Filthy Irish pigs" was heard. Anyone with even a titter of understanding would have found the deadly silence which followed that remark far more frightening than the noise. My friend's informant jumped out of bed and began to pack quickly. Before he had his clothes on there was a sudden rush of feet, the door burst open and with a soaring roar of "Over the bar, Mayo", the cock-lodger was hurled over the banisters and down the well of the stairs.

What happened afterwards, my friend's informant did not really know. In his own expressive phrase, "Níor fhan mé le torann na gcos" (I did not wait to hear the sound of my own footsteps). He rushed down the stairs, jumped over the prone Welshman and the shrieking landlady and headed for yet another temporary nest. I would be greatly surprised if the Mayomen had not been hot on his heels.

My own succession of boring jobs in London need not be elaborated on. The last one was as a night-porter in a small hotel off Russell Square. I took the job in an attempt to save money by sleeping all day and working all night when there would be no opportunity of spending very much. The hotel was frequented by jockeys who went to the Turkish Baths around the corner to lose weight. They were a jolly crowd but the owners of the hotel were not. They were mean and spiteful and, as ill-luck would have it, Welsh. By the time I decided to find work where I would have no means at all of spending money, I was laying the foundation of a strong prejudice against my so-called Celtic cousins.

As far as my financial capability to get there was concerned, Rome had by now moved east of Istanbul; after that there was the small matter of getting home again. I had to get out of London and the only logical solution seemed a job at sea.

I took a train to Grimsby, went to the docks and after lying ferociously about my experience aboard steam-trawlers (which was non-existent), I signed as a deckhand/learner with the firm of Alexander Sleight, on the North Sea trawler *Recordo*, for a twelve to fourteen day trip to the Dogger Bank.

The second thoughts which usually come after I have committed myself to an irrevocable course of action were, on this occasion, futile. This did not mean that I did not entertain them. After a couple of days I longed for all the jobs I had walked away from in London — particularly the last one, which from the deck of this rusty tub now seemed like a week at Galway Races.

It was not that the work was particularly hard; or that the fo'c'sle where we slept was dank and dirty; or that we only got broken sleep by day and by night; or that we lacked even a toilet and had to perch precariously on the rail like monkeys, when the weather permitted, and crouch in the coal, when it did not; but that I had never before found myself isolated in the company of ten men whose combined vocabulary seemed not to exceed five hundred words — including the seven or eight obscenities which were stuck in between every second one of them.

But I had one friend aboard, a little Glaswegian called Jimmy Smith who was the second engineer. He was as full of contempt for the rest of the crew as I was but he warned me to keep my lip buttoned while at sea, and speak only when spoken to. Although not much older than myself, he had been reared much harder and left home younger. He told hilarious stories about stoning Orange marches in Glasgow, and sure enough, he could hit a seagull with a lump of coal nine shots out of ten.

After two trips I had recovered the money I spent in London and as I spent my thirty-six hours ashore, sleeping and washing my clothes in the Mission, or in Cleethorpes with Smith, who was married to a hairdresser there, I was beginning to experience that feeling of virtue which almost always signals a fall. I even made myself popular with one of the older deckhands, who was illiterate, by reading him passages from some of the dirty books which, with a bundle of old speedway magazines, composed the fo'c'sle library.

He was particularly fond of one called *Hot Dames on Cold Slabs* by Hank Janson. By present-day standards it would be fit for a school library, but the year after I was in Grimsby the publishers and author were prosecuted by the police. However, Hank Janson was outside the jurisdiction. He was a retired English schoolmaster, living in San Sebastian and supplementing his small pension by writing these preposterous books.

In return for this favour the old deckhand, who had spent all his life from the age of eleven fishing for this company, told me stories about the Sleight empire and how it started with a donkey-cartload of cockles and periwinkles, from the beach outside the town, and ended with a fleet of trawlers and streets of houses. The proudest moment of the poor man's life was when one of the Sleights, who was a Conservative member of parliament, was knighted for services rendered.

He was a poor talker. He would remind you of a door that was bolted for years and now moved with difficulty on corroded hinges. And he came to mind, years later, when I heard Séamus Kavanagh in Radio Eireann tell the story of two tramps on O'Connell Bridge watching an elderly man being driven past in a Rolls Royce.

"It's Kilmartin the bookie," said one of them.

"And isn't he a credit to us," said the other.

At the end of the third trip, after a row with the chief engineer about Irish neutrality during the war and all the sailors that lost their lives because of our stupid pro-German policies, I had to leave and sign off. The chief engineer was the only truly bigoted anti-Irish Englishman I met in my travels that summer and he eventually succeeded in getting me to lose my temper. He was too old to hit, but I was scrubbing the cabin floor at the time and I doused him with the bucket of water and carbolic soap. I felt the better of it, although we were steaming up the Humber when it happened. I made a point of shaking hands with all hands as I left the *Recordo* for the last time but the old bigot pretended to be afraid of me and refused to come out of his cabin. That made me feel even better.

Leaving Grimsby and heading inland by train, I moved through a succession of sleepy but beautifully-preserved towns before taking a job on a farm belonging to The Cambridge Institute of Agriculture. Sometimes, when in the right mood and company, I would mention my period in Cambridge to create another impression.

It was a research farm, but my part in its activities was confined to driving equipment from one area to another at very slow speed in a jeep. But while the speed was in keeping with my driving ability, the pay corresponded to the simplicity of the work and was not sufficient to maintain my standard of life ashore.

In places like Cambridge, where there were not a lot of Irish, it was easy to find the pub where they gathered, as it was usually the one most English drinkers avoided and thus became known locally as the Irish pub. Most of the Irish in the area at the time worked for farmers and a lot of them came from Mayo, Roscommon and east Galway. Having been out of touch with home and out of contact with Irish people, for some time, I was quickly assailed by pangs of homesickness and, as in the Beckett story, decided that although I had missed the hurling I would be there to see Mayo play Louth in football. I collected my last measly pay packet and headed for home.

This time I was determined to side-step the fleshpots of London and so allowed myself only one night to visit a few places where exiles gathered. Mayomen were terribly conspicuous that September, but not one person from Louth did I see or hear. Every second Mayoman was either going, or trying to make up his mind to go, to see the county triumph for the first time since 1936.

And I noticed, not for the last time, how these interminable discussions and arguments about games they had never seen and knew nothing about made the Irish seem strange to the English, despite having a language in common. The fact that these games were only played by the Irish made them seem quaint, to those favourably disposed, or plain daft, to those who were not. (Did I hear someone mutter, "As if we didn't have it in our own house?") Of course, at this stage, I only knew the working-class Irish in Britain.

Back at UCG the struggle to keep up the pretence of going to lectures became even harder. Three of us took up residence in the Castle Hotel, in Abbeygate Street, right in the centre of town and only a stone's throw from the docks. Now the distractions were nearer at hand. To get to college I passed the Four Corners, and in those days if there was an islander in town you found him by standing there for a few minutes.

After that there was the Courthouse, near the Salmon Weir Bridge, a bilingual institution infinitely more entertaining than the university and one could salve an uneasy conscience by going for a browse in the County Library upstairs during a dull case. Ever more frequently I found myself strolling back to the Castle Hotel, for lunch or tea, my notebooks still under my arm, not having been near college at all.

One found out a lot about life in Galway and its hinterland in the court and, as a guard once said to me sarcastically, my long hours in the public gallery must have been a great help when the time came for me to play a more central role in the court's proceedings.

I attended the hearing of a seduction case in which it was stated in evidence that the accused, a soldier in the 1st Irish-Speaking Battalion, had used his army great-coat as a make-shift bed. The District Justice, who was an advanced patriot and puritan, remarked that this was a scandalous use for a garment that was, as he put it, dedicated to Pearse. The accused, who did not understand the allusion but who thought he was also being accused of larceny, roared, "Oh, no! It was not Pearse's coat, your Honour, but my own."

He later caused the court to explode with laughter, which the Justice could not control, when he excused the seduction in words which are well-remembered in Galway: "Is amhlaidh a sciorr sé isteach i nganfhios dom, a dhuine uasail." ("It slipped in unknown to me, sir.")

A minor, giving evidence in a similar case, was adamant that the action took place for the first time, between ten and half past ten at night. Counsel for the defence was suspicious of this degree of accuracy until he was demolished by the simplicity of her reply, "I am absolutely sure, because the news in Irish was on the radio." Small wonder that in any contest between a lecture on Anglo-Saxon verbs and the Courthouse there could only be one winner.

Myles na Gopaleen wrote frequently, at this time, in his column in *The Irish Times*, attacking violence at football and hurling matches and the GAA's reluctance to deal firmly with it by calling in the Garda Síochána to arrest and charge the miscreants. He had great fun during the making of the film, *The Rising of the Moon*, in the mid-fifties, when the Clare County Board of the GAA objected to a scene that was being shot in Kilkee. It showed a team coming home from a match, some on stretchers, some on crutches, all bandaged and bloodstained.

Myles, who was a careful reader of the local papers, pounced on a referee's report which was discussed at a recent County Board meeting and reported in the *Clare Champion*. Myles re-published extracts in his own column, particularly the part in which the referee (who happened to be a priest) described how a player approached him holding in his hand the severed portion of his ear. Myles wanted to know why the GAA did not banish the player responsible from its ranks forever, instead of protesting foolishly about something far less damaging than what seemed to be tolerated by the Association.

Rough and sometimes brutal hurling was common enough in those years. It was usually confined to the lower grades of club hurling, or to meetings of parish teams with a long history of spites and spleens behind them. I saw it too in some of the Munster Finals I now see described as "great", very often by people who did not see them. The GAA's attitude to it was that of the three little monkeys who neither see, speak nor hear evil. This did a lot to bring the game into disrepute, particularly with parents who worried about injuries to their children.

Hurling is much cleaner nowadays but the GAA's attitude to well-publicised incidents of violence has not changed all that much. At most the monkeys may have lifted a finger or two, but they still have to remove their hands completely.

One day in court there was what seemed, at first sight, a fairly ordinary case of assault. A man had walked into a public house, outside the city, and addressed two customers who were sitting drinking pints and minding their own business, with the words, "Ballindooley, my bollocks! Everything above the grass but the thistles."

The two customers put down their pints and laying their hands upon the speaker, did severe damage to his person. The remark, which may seem as enigmatic to you as it did to me when I first heard it, referred to a junior hurling match in which Ballindooley were reputed to have followed the advice of a famous Tipperary hurler when his team was in trouble: "Hurl away and don't mind the ball." The speaker of the offending words was one of those who had suffered. He was obviously one of those men who are born to suffer.

As was the case elsewhere, there were two kinds of hurling played in Galway: good class and poor class. While good hurling sometimes erupted in disorder, bad hurlers usually compensated for lack of speed or skill by hard and previous pulling and other forms of intimidation and foul play. Junior hurling everywhere was notoriously dirty in those times. It was the purgatory where old and battered hurlers, lingering on before retirement, tried to maim the younger ones, waiting for release into senior ranks. Never in my life did I hear it said of anyone that he was a great junior, but every county in Ireland seemed to claim the dirtiest junior footballer or hurler that ever cracked a skull or broke a kneecap.

There were, of course, the running feuds that appealed so much to my friends who tended the street corners and who longed for "the bit of slashing above in the Sportsground" to bring a ray of sunshine into the tedium of a dull Sunday.

Very often these feuds flourished in the proximity of adjoining parishes, such as Castlegar and Turloughmore in Galway, or Clarecastle and Newmarket-on-Fergus in Clare, and may have had their roots in old ancestral battles far removed from hurling. Sometimes they stemmed from more recent incidents connected with the game: a bad injury, objections and counter-objections, a player who switched allegiance in the hope of winning a medal, "unfinished business" from a previous encounter, or deliberate trouble-making on the sideline from which so many people seem to derive great pleasure. For good or ill, these wars and rumours of wars added to local interest and to the ever-accumulating folklore.

In my own experience, one was more likely to find rougher play and more violence in places where county teams had least hope of winning even a provincial title. The county championships were therefore somewhat over-valued and this affected standards of play and behaviour. The best players in some of these counties were literally kicked and belted out of the game in ways which would cause those responsible to be regarded as blackguards, in counties where the players they injured would be essential to the success of the county team: not that this consideration, in itself, is a guarantee of immunity from blackguardism, but it does help.

As we have seen, the Galway hurlers seemed to be heading for that long-awaited All-Ireland between the midforties and the early fifties, and interest in hurling in the county was intense. During my student years I do not seem to have seen very much club football, or indeed any football at all apart from one Sigerson Cup competition (when one felt in duty bound to go along and cheer for UCG) and a few National League matches. But even when the county team was in the doldrums, attendances at county hurling finals were always bigger than at county football finals, and the heartland of Galway football lay far away from the city in those years.

Despite the fact that I only saw the matches that were played in the Sportsground, I did see some of the best players ever to wear the county colours, in action for either club, county or province. Seán Duggan was one of the best goalkeepers in the country and he and his brothers, Jimmy and Paddy (Mogan) were to Galway then what the Connollys were to become thirty years later, with greater success. Then there were Joe Salmon, John Killeen, Billy Duffy (who could have become the best centre-half back of his day had emigration not stunted his development), Josie and Stephen Gallagher, Inky Flaherty, Johnny Molloy, Mickey Burke and Father Paddy Gantley.

Father Gantley had a peculiar career with Galway, for after his ordination in the SMA he had to play as Paddy Gardiner in an effort to circumvent the ecclesiastical ban on priests playing hurling or football at county, and sometimes even club, level. The reasons for the ban are not clear but can be taken as another sign of the times. Even as Paddy Gardiner, Father Gantley had problems and eventually had to give up playing for Galway, but after his order transferred him to Cork he won a county championship there with St Finbarr's.

Poor Bishop Browne of Galway keeps on coming into the action despite my best intentions. He was much blamed for not shutting his eyes to what was not really his business, and depriving the county of a really good hurler. But, in fairness to the Bishop, the rule was applied in most dioceses at the time and long before.

The most celebrated case of this ecclesiastical ban concerns a Kerry footballer named Richard Prendiville. He was a student in All-Hallows and had returned to his studies when Kerry were to play Dublin in the All-Ireland final in 1924. Great pressure was put on the college authorities to let him out to play the match. I have heard it said that the Bishop of Kerry was asked to intervene on behalf of the County Board and Kerry patriotism, but to no avail.

But the call of the Kingdom took precedence over all other calls, as far as young Prendiville was concerned, and out he went and played and won.

He then finished his studies elsewhere, was ordained a priest and went to Australia. In 1946, Dr Richard Prendiville, now Archbishop of Perth, re-visited the scene of his past success and threw in the ball to start the All-Ireland final.

Not all such stories have a happy ending. In Meath you will still meet people who believe it was Kildare that informed on a priest who was playing football for them under an assumed name, and that Kildare's punishment for this base betrayal is plain for all to see. This is an example of fact being transformed into inaccurate folklore with a moral tagged on to its tail. Father Michael McManus did indeed play football with Meath, before and after his ordination in the Irish College in Paris. He was an outstanding player and was playing so well that the County Board decided to take the Bishop into their confidence, sooner rather than later, and sent a delegation to the Palace to make a clean breast of it.

The Bishop listened and then said, sadly, that he knew Father McManus was playing, but not officially. Now that he knew officially he had no choice but to forbid him to play in the future. Kildare seem to have been blamed because it was against them Father McManus happened to play his last game for Meath.

For those clerics who were willing to run the risk of the ecclesiastical ban there were other hazards. In Limerick I heard a story of a match in which an unknown but clearly talented player was being given a very rough time indeed by his marker. As well as pulling wildly, before the ball arrived, and a split second after it had gone again, he subjected his opponent to a litany of abuse and obscenity.

At half-time an official took him aside and said, "You'd better take it easy: your man is a priest." The abusive player was shocked and before the match resumed he went up to the priest, offered his hand, and said, "I'm terribly sorry about that, Father. Sure I thought you were only a Christian Brother."

Winning the National League Hurling final in 1951, at home against Wexford and away against New York, seemed like another step towards the All-Ireland. I travelled to Dublin full of foreboding and returned elated and full of CIE stout to the gills. In victory, all the long bicycle rides to one defeat after another began to seem like part of the necessary preparation for success. To those accustomed to many defeats, victory is particularly satisfying.

After the team returned from America, Miko McInerney was very generous with the presents homesick and sentimental Galwegians had pressed on the Galway players with instructions to drink their health in the Old Malt House, Larry Hynes', McNamara's or whatever their own favourite pub happened to be. That is one of my last pleasant memories before all my problems seemed to hatch simultaneously and scurry away beyond reach and out of control.

Apart from the fact that it was a very unexciting year, considerations of vanity also prompt me to tip-toe through the period after I shied away from my final examinations, forfeited my scholarship and my temporary independence, and returned to Aran to spend my first winter there since I was fourteen — and my last.

The time was spent being sorry for myself: building stone walls to shelter my mother's flower-beds; playing the accordion in the dance hall for the diminishing group of young people who were following their friends into exile; losing the last lingering desire to sit the examinations in Autumn and prove my mental stability by getting an honours degree; telling colourful lies to the more inquisitive neighbours who asked me cheerfully why my holidays seemed to last forever; running out of books and being reduced to reading Dr. O'Brien's heap of back numbers of *Psychic News*, (to which he was given a life subscription by an English Spiritualist grateful for attention received after falling over a wall while trying to communicate with someone or other near Dún Dubh Chathair) and thereby causing my parents much concern; reading the *Connacht Tribune* and missing all the films and the matches, as well as the dances which I would not attend had I still been in Galway.

I found some relief in corresponding with my friend Jim O'Halloran, who had also baled out of the Castle Hotel and UCG in much the same condition as myself and had sought sanctuary in London. Most of the letters were on the general topic, "Where do we go from here?"

In the summer of 1952 the national newspapers closed because of a strike that lasted long enough to cause this addict to have withdrawal symptoms. My father went to Galway one weekend and was instructed to bring home every paper and periodical in sight, which he did. Included in the bundle was *Inniu*, which was not read in Aran, and being really in a bad way I even scrutinised the advertisements. One of these sent a shock to the roots of my hair.

Here it was: this was the way out of my predicament. It did smack a bit of the Furry Glen Publishing Company, but it did seem to possess cultural and mechanical – not to mention financial – advantages unknown to the poor pedlars of my youth.

An organisation called Comhdháil Náisiúnta na Gaeilge, about which I knew very little except that Earnán de Blaghd was its President, was looking for a travelling book-salesman and organiser who would travel the country and display its wares, as well as promoting the language in a variety of unspecified ways. Salary seemed more than adequate to my needs and subsistence and travel allowance would be paid, as well as commission on sales.

I would have cheerfully taken my chance with the subsistence and commission, but I resolved to land this job even if I had to lie my way into it. So I spent days concocting a spurious "national record", trying to make it as plausible as possible by straining out every strand that ever connected me with the language movement — like a little boy trying to make his last morsel of gum last as long as possible by drawing it in and out of his mouth.

My short spell with an Cumann Eigse agus Seanachais in UCG was extended and embellished, I took a chance and "published" a story which had been rejected by a college magazine, then went wild and claimed membership of An Réalt, on the strength of attending some of their céilithe in Aras na nGael, in Dominic St — my interest in this organisation lay in the vain hope of getting a sneaky feel of one of their less pious members. (An Réalt was the Irish-speaking branch of the Legion of Mary and I felt that the organisation owed me a good turn.)

After much re-writing, my first serious creative composition was dispatched and my spirits rose, for the first time in a year, when I was called for an interview. Patrick Kavanagh, in one of his essays, describes how the trainer of his local team in Monaghan would not let the players touch a ball for a week before the county final, as he wanted them to be "ball hungry". So "job hungry" was I that year that I took off for Dublin almost a full week before the interview.

I stayed with Liam, who had now settled in a flat near Baggot St Bridge and was putting the finishing touches to his collection of short stories, *Dúil*. He was possessed by a new enthusiasm and I happened to fit perfectly into it. Giving me what I later classified as his "Head Centre look" he told me he had been busily engaged in collecting information on the executive of Comhdháil Náisiúnta na Gaeilge, who would be interviewing me, and that great cunning and resourcefulness was called for if I was to get this most desirable job.

Was it not significant that one of my tasks would be to promote his own first book in Irish? This had not occurred to me, but I agreed that it was. In my anxiety I was becoming superstitious. He then placed a total ban on drinking and late nights until the task was completed. Every evening we met and went to the cinema and after supper, when I was allowed one glass of wine, we returned to the flat and had a mock interview, on the lines of that hilarious episode in *Tarry Flynn*.

Liam played Earnán de Blaghd with great gusto, asking questions like, "I see! Your Uncle Liam once seized the Rotunda and declared some sort of an Irish Soviet. What are his politics now?" The answer to this most unlikely question was, "We don't often discuss politics, but I have heard him speak approvingly of Franco and Peron." This would please de Blaghd and the other couple of closet fascists who were on the board, according to Liam's information.

He would then play the only member of the board he actually knew, Seán Sáirséal O hEigeartaigh, who was publishing *Dúil* and who was going to ask all the penetrating questions and it was up to me to play to my strength and impress the rest of the board. Then there was another very important matter which, according to Liam, was bound to be mentioned. He had it on the best authority that the gentleman who would have the task of supervising my work, if I got the job, had already been sniffing out my trail in Galway. I had to be prepared for this, and there was to be no foolish retreat into falsehood. This part of the preparation struck me as fringing on lunacy but I kept my thoughts to myself.

I was dispatched to the interview on a Friday night, programmed and prettied up in some of Liam's best clothes. Now I was on my own and Liam relieved his nervousness by going on a blinder with Seán O Sullivan, the painter, and getting barred (as I later heard) from an astonishing number of pubs between Dawson Street and Grafton Street.

I was the last one called for interview and to my complete amazement it progressed roughly but uncannily along the lines of my rehearsals. Earnán de Blaghd, whom I recognised from press photographs, asked the difficult questions. One of them was so convoluted in its purpose that I still remember it:

Would I prefer to sell one book to an obviously enthusiastic reader or sell five to a parish priest (why the hell a parish priest? I asked myself) who was going to throw them on a shelf and not read them at all?

I was beginning to flounder and to add to my difficulty an irreverent parody, composed by a teacher in Clare who had it in for de Blaghd for cutting teachers' salaries when Minister for Finance, came annoyingly to mind:

Hell to thee, Blythe spirit
Man thou never wert but Devil.

The lifebelt was thrown by a handsome man with gentle eyes and a musical voice, who turned the questioning towards contemporary writing in Irish and I could feel the mood of the board changing in my favour and my own confidence strengthened accordingly. This was my first meeting with Seán O hEigeartaigh, an exceptional man of many parts for whose company I was later to work and whose early death affected me as would a brother's.

Then, just as the interview seemed to be coming to its logical conclusion, with me in a relaxed mood, a hospital pass was hurled at me. It came from a grey-haired man who had not spoken all through the interview, but who had never once taken his eyes off me, and who waited until I began to move my chair before he let fly, "Just a last little point, do you drink?" I could hardly believe it.

During my very short career as an amateur actor in Taibhdhearc na Gaillimhe, no less a person than Ria Mooney told me that I was probably the most wooden person she ever attempted to direct on a stage. Had she been present in that room she would have had reason to revise that opinion and admit that my best performances were given under pressure in real life.

"Indeed, I do," I smiled sweetly, "I love a glass of wine with a meal at night."

Brian Mac Cafaid, with whom I was destined to play hide-and-go-seek for the next two years, did not move a muscle either, but his eyes spoke volumes and he had put his reservation on the record.

The following day I got a call telling me that I had been successful and Liam took me on a pub-crawl, through friendly hostelries, introducing me as the nephew who only drank wine with meals and roaring with laughter.

Naturally, I arrived home with a great welcome for myself which was reciprocated warmly by my father and more tepidly by my mother. Now that I had actually got the job, she felt free to let some air out of my almost newly-acquired tyres.

We went for a walk one evening, down by the shore-road past Mainistir and Eochaill, and she began to tell me parables about people who found themselves working for committees composed of people who were ostensibly working for the same cause but were really engaged in achieving gains for one faction at the expense of another. The unfortunate employee ended by being a rope in a tug-of-war, and while none of them seemed to have committed suicide, there were a few bad mental breakdowns . . .

She then went off on another tack. These people who wanted everyone to speak Irish. . . . Why was it that their own families either did not speak it at all, or else ceased to speak it once they left home and their fanatical parents behind them? She hoped I would not become a fanatic like some of the enthusiasts she knew in Belfast, where she had trained and taught.

As always, my mother was pretending to shoot at various targets and actually hitting others which were not mentioned at all. She was greatly disappointed that I had thrown college overboard and her way of letting me know was to strip all the cultural gilt off this job and leave me exposed as a mere commercial traveller, a breed whose dissolute behaviour in hotels, gross appetites and total lack of any useful role in society put them even lower on my mother's social register than policemen, process-servers and parish priests.

But having exposed me to that blast of stern reality, she wished me luck and stood for a long time on the head of Kilronan pier waving to me as I sailed happily away to soldier among the great Gaels of Ireland.

8

Comhdháil Náisiúnta na Gaeilge was founded at the prompting of Éamon de Valera, in the mid-forties, to co-ordinate the work of the various Irish language organisations. That sounds like a reasonable and simple objective but, with de Valera, very few things were straightforward, whatever about being reasonable.

Since coming into power in 1932 de Valera had enjoyed a fairly cosy relationship with the Gaelic League, which was the only language organisation in existence and carried a fair amount of clout. During the war, new organisations were founded by young people who were tired of listening to the patriarchs of the Gaelic League telling them that they had de Valera by the ear and that all would be well if the young people had patience. Some of these new organisations founded newspapers and periodicals of their own, held street meetings, threatened to get involved in politics and social issues, and attacked the Gaelic League for behaving like a branch of Fianna Fáil.

De Valera was unhappy with this breach of the rules of the game and it is said that one of his advisors on language affairs, An Seabhac, recommended that a co-ordinating body be set up, given an annual grant and, with the help of God, be controlled by the right people who would contain the more revolutionary elements in the fullness of time. I doubt if de Valera needed much convincing. A friend of mine was fond of saying that Dev was a great one for putting "all his Basques in one exit", keeping a sharp eye on their comings and goings and controlling them with a balanced application of carrots and kicks. Be that as it may, Comhdháil Náisiúnta na Gaeilge was launched at a meeting in the Mansion House at which the Catholic Archbishop of Dublin, John Charles McQuaid, said that the Irish language was the shrine that contained our religion. How this curious sentiment was received by the many non-Catholics present has not been recorded.

And with God's help — and some sleight of hand which would have drawn tears of envy from the eyes of a three-card-trick-man — the new organisation was indeed controlled by the right people. The disappointed ones went away to skulk in their tents and plot.

Like most new organisations An Chomhdháil sought an early spectacular success to impress friend and foe alike. A map of Ireland was examined by a committee and it was decided to revive Irish in an area where it had recently given way to English as a first language of communication. They homed in on an area of East Cork which would be roughly enclosed by a triangle made by lines connecting Fermoy, Youghal, Ballycotton and Fermoy.

They then employed five or six young organisers and placed them strategically throughout this region, ordering them to get on with the job, under the supervision of Brian Mac Cafaid. It was never made clear to the young men how this linguistic miracle was going to be achieved. But committees need reports and figures on which to feed, and to provide An Chomhdháil with a yardstick, success or failure was assessed by the number of meetings the organisers convened every week and the number of committees that resulted from these meetings.

To keep them in a state of constant agitation, Brian Mac Cafaid descended on them from Dublin, unannounced and at irregular intervals in his car, to find out how many meetings they had organised for that particular day. As soon as he was sighted, the organiser concerned would go to the nearest post office and send a simple telegram to his colleagues, "Cú chugat" (Hound approaches).

Once, Annraoi Ó Liatháin, who was later to become President of the Gaelic League himself, was caught "meet-ingless" and very much on the wrong foot. Keeping his nerve as best he could he took Brian for a drive along a remote country road, praying hard, and was lucky enough to come on a dimly-lighted schoolhouse where a meeting was indeed in progress. Rushing in to the startled chairman, Annraoi pleaded with him to allow his slightly deranged boss to address the meeting for a few minutes, or else that he would almost certainly lose his job.

The chairman was too startled to refuse and Brian was ushered in and told to be as brief as possible, as it was Annraoi's policy to give his local committees complete autonomy. Brian launched into his stock speech which combined quotations from Pearse and other assorted patriots with aphorisms praising Irish at the expense of English. As soon as he drew a long breath Annraoi led a round of applause and ushered Brian out to the car. Doubling back on some pretext, with the intention of thanking the unknown chairman for having saved his bacon, Annraoi was stopped in his tracks at the door by the sound of an angry voice being directed at his benefactor:

"What in the name of Jasus has all that shite to do with Rural Electrification?"

Almost thirty years after this absurd adventure was abandoned I found myself in the southern part of this region, in Ballymacoda, in my capacity as a television reporter, during a by-election. Tom O'Donnell, the then Minister for the Gaeltacht, at a meeting after mass, repeated his promise to include the place in the official Gaeltacht if the people continued to attend their Irish classes and became fluent. We filmed one of the classes, and the teacher wrote on the blackboard, for the benefit of class and camera, that the Irish language was the greatest possible defence against atheistic Communism. This film is in the archives of RTE and should be good for a laugh when we are all dead and gone.

One of those coups, much beloved of Irish revolutionaries who confuse them with positive action, replaced the committee of Good Gaelic Leaguers. A consortium of organisations opposed to the Gaelic League, with Earnán de Blaghd as an agreed President, took over An Chomhdháil. The deposed ones went away in a huff and decided that their objectives were best achieved in isolation. This is roughly where I came in. My total ignorance of Irish language organisations and politics was regarded as extraordinary by some and as a definite mark in my favour by others. Nobody came to the simple but correct conclusion that I needed a bloody job and did not care very much what it entailed.

I was also ignorant in a much more important respect. One of my most brazen lies, in my application and in my interview, concerned my ability to drive. Apart from the short period spent driving a jeep slowly across level fields in Cambridge, I had no experience at all of driving anything more complex than a bicycle, or a pony and cart, on a public road. So, as soon as I arrived back in Dublin, I enrolled in the O'Connell Bridge School of Motoring and tried to overtake my lies.

I doubt very much if I would have lasted a week in the job had I not been given into the care of the man who had already spent a year doing the work and with whom I was eventually going to share the island of Ireland for the purpose of selling and promoting Irish books. This was going to happen when my new Volkswagen van was fitted with shelves and suitably inscribed, so as to render me as conspicuous on the roads as an advance agent for a circus.

When I was introduced to Tomás Mac Gabhann I realised that this was a man who could be trusted with the secret of my shortcomings. We went to a pub around the corner from the office, in 29 Lower O'Connell Street, and I told him everything. His hearty laughter, which was to raise my spirits on so many occasions in the future, assured me that there was nothing wrong which could not be remedied discreetly. We were to work together for a few months, using his van, and by the time we parted, to work north and south of a line from Dublin to Galway, he would see to it that I would be master of all the necessary skills, driving included.

He cheered me greatly by telling me that I seemed to possess the degree of lunacy necessary for survival in the strange world of which I was now to become a part. With considerable help from him I was to survive for almost two years before I exceeded the limit and was forced to go on the run.

For most of the next two years I lived in hotels. When the commercial travellers began to head towards their homes on Fridays, I either stayed where I was or else moved to another hotel closer to the following week's work. Travelling to and from home in Inis Mór was impossible, but even if it were not, the pattern of my new life was far too fascinating to break.

Frequently I was the only one staying in a hotel during the weekend and this led to many interesting, but sometimes complicated, relationships. A disapproving friend described my travels through Ireland at this time as unsteady movement from barmaid to barmaid. But I was enjoying myself immensely and was determined to exploit to the full this golden opportunity to explore every corner of Ireland that contained a school and not let the essential dreariness of the work affect my enjoyment of the hours of leisure.

The commercial travellers did not know what to make of me and refused to accept me as one of the fraternity at all. In one way this was a relief for I was beginning to find out that my mother's acid comments on the members of that profession were only too accurate. However, to qualify for the commercial rate in some hotels it was necessary to sit at the table in the dining-room reserved for commercials. I described myself as a book salesman, but my emerald green van with blue and gold inscriptions along its sides and across its snout (and in the Irish language, for God's sake!) put me firmly out of lodge. The only saving grace was the amount of writing I sometimes had to do in the commercial room. That signified that I was getting orders and orders meant money. If they only knew that I was merely reporting on the state of Irish in the various towns I passed through they would have been reduced to helpless laughter.

The conversation at the commercials' table was so terribly boring and repetitive that I actually remember the only incident that made me laugh during meal-times. One traveller from Limerick, who seemed to read nothing but digests and who was forever scrutinising the cutlery for specks of dirt, and bullying the waitresses – in the same way, I later found out, his wife bullied him when he was at home – acted the part of senior knight of the road in the hotels he stayed in. The bane of his life was a traveller for a Dublin firm of confectioners who behaved like a caricature of a commercial traveller in a bad play or film.

This character always looked as if someone had thrown his clothes at him with a pitchfork, he played poker and drank gin into the small hours every night, was forever sneaking into bedrooms and tumbling chambermaids of all ages on to beds and smoked one cigarette after another, even during meals.

One morning in Clonmel he came to breakfast with cracked eyes, like the cartoon cat that has been hit on the head with a hammer, and a hacking cough that caused him to gasp for breath. The elder knight took up the *Reader's Digest* and began to read aloud from an article which described experiments on rats in some laboratory in America. The rats were injected with ever-increasing amounts of nicotine until they developed hideous tumours which eventually caused them to die squealing. Even my own strong stomach was beginning to heave and others at the table began to plead for mercy.

When he came to the end he put down the magazine and said to the dissolute one, who had now lit another cigarette, "Now, Mr Browne, doesn't that make you think?"

"It certainly does," said Browne agreeably, "I think bloody rats shouldn't smoke."

Patrick Kavanagh has written that it is true in a way that no man can adequately describe Irish life who ignores the GAA because football runs women a hard race as a topic for conversation. Dónal Foley often wondered what most of his friends would be talking about, particularly between June and October, had Cusack not founded the GAA.

My travels with An Chomhdháil added to my knowledge of Ireland in various ways. They even enabled me to visit the scenes of some of my favourite murders. I was somewhat tactless in those days and I still feel embarrassed at the memory of the deadly silence that followed my casual enquiry, in a Waterville pub, as to the exact location of what was known nationally as "The Cá bhFuil Sé" murder. But it did teach me to be a little more circumspect in the future.

My area included some of the great traditional football areas, as well as areas where one never saw a football: places like south Kilkenny where a ball was automatically hit with a hurley. I was becoming familiar with the hurling map of Ireland, the football map and the areas where both games flourished. Having known Offaly then, for instance, makes me more appreciative of the progress which has since made that county so successful in both codes — particularly as I am familiar with the tiny area where hurling is played traditionally and also with the missing slice of that area which was "stolen" by Tipperary.

Having seen what were considered to be rough matches in Galway I was taken aback by the absolute ferocity of club hurling and football in other counties. One match in Wicklow scared me out of a year's growth. I had not realised that one part of a county could regard another part almost as enemy territory. Perhaps it was because of the mountains that divided them, but it produced the most protracted running fight I have ever seen, and many columns of letters in the local paper for weeks afterwards.

Because of the circles I moved in, and the views I held, I was constantly involved in arguments about the Ban. One Sunday in Limerick as I left a dreadful soccer match in the Market Fields, I came face to face with Seán South who took me severely to task for not having attended instead a Manchester Martyrs Commemoration, from which he was returning. He then proceeded to attack the GAA for not doing enough for the Irish language. On one of my last visits to the Shamrock Rovers ground, to see them play Limerick, one of the songs the Limerick supporters sang was "Seán South of Garryowen".

But I was still keeping an eye on those Galway hurlers and in 1953, enjoying my new mobility, set out from Galway to see them play Kilkenny in the All-Ireland semi-final in Croke Park. The previous year they were considered unlucky, yet again, to lose to Cork in the semi-final in Limerick. I persuaded myself that bad luck needs only time to turn.

On my way into Ballinasloe I got a puncture, and by the time I found a garage that was prepared to mend it on a Sunday, it was too late to continue. When I arrived back in Galway there was a buzz in the streets. Galway had won by a point. To make it even better it was a lucky win, and for the first time since I was born the hurlers had reached the final. Feeling very lucky now, I arranged to be in Galway on the first weekend in September to take my father and five other friends from home to the match.

We travelled up at the crack of dawn, four sitting on borrowed chairs in the back among the books, and were among the first thousand in the queue for sideline seats. The attendance that day was 72,000 but there was no crush where we found seats, directly on the twenty-one yard line, at the Canal End on the Hogan Stand side of the field.

After a very bad first half, during which the Cork rearguard of Creedon, O'Shaughnessy, Lyons and O'Riordan held the Galway full forward line in a vice, Galway came out and surprised even their most optimistic followers by cutting Cork's four point lead to level scores in a short spell of furious hurling. They were beaten by four points in the end, mainly because they did not have enough scoring forwards. For once, Josie Gallagher, who was picked out of his best position, and on whose individual brilliance the team relied so much, had what was for him a quiet hour.

It was a hard match, particularly in the last quarter, played in intense heat and as P.D. Mehigan (Pato) wrote in *The Irish Times* on the following Monday: "Tired men were inclined to use their hurleys over much."

But nothing that we saw in Croke Park prepared us for the controversy that blew up on Monday, reached gale force on Wednesday and raged like a hurricane for weeks. Although more than thirty years have passed, the affair is still discussed, and it ensured that the name of Mickey Burke is coupled in the folklore of hurling with that of Christy Ring.

The brief clash occurred in the second half after Ring had moved to midfield where Joe Salmon and Billy Duffy were gaining the upper hand for Galway. Burke, the Galway captain, who had been policing Ring in the right half back position (with much of the same success he enjoyed in Limerick the previous year), followed Ring to midfield.

It was an ill-advised move in more ways than one: it upset the rhythm of Galway's play; the balance of the team, which had at last settled down, was upset; and it led to the incident in which Burke received an injury to his face and mouth. To put it less euphemistically, Ring, irritated by the constant proximity of Burke, hit him a belt in the face.

Val Dorgan, in his book on Christy Ring, has devoted a chapter to the incident and when Paddy Downey's biography of Ring is published we are bound to get another — or perhaps the same — version of what actually happened. When I later worked with Christy Ring on the commentary for Louis Marcus' film on him, the subject was avoided so pointedly that at times Mickey Burke seemed to be hovering over our heads.

Maurice Gorham, Director of Radio Éireann, was the only one I met who actually saw the blow delivered. He was on the Cusack Stand and kept his eye on the pair when play moved away from them. He then saw Ring turn and give Burke a dig of his hurley in the jaw or mouth and Burke went down, although he did finish the game — something that Ring emphasised to people who dared ask him what actually happened.

My own feeling, at the time and ever since, is that the Galway County Board made a meal out of the incident. In the first place, if Burke followed Ring to midfield without instruction from the sideline, as he told Raymond Smith years later, the selectors should have sent him back to his place immediately. Secondly, they should have exercised some control over the players who engaged in fairday behaviour in Barry's Hotel and the Gresham Hotel the following day. They should certainly have resisted the temptation to strike a special medal for Burke, which was like setting up a Provisional Central Council, instead of pressing the real Central Council for a full enquiry into the circumstances of Burke's injuries.

It was to be expected that the Cork County Board, the Cork players and *The Cork Examiner* would close ranks and try to cloak the original incident in the smoke of its aftermath. It is scarcely necessary to add (but out of sheer badness of mind I am going to add it anyway) that the courage, fearlessness and devotion to truth and fair play which the GAA never displays on such occasions were also conspicuous by their absence in 1953.

Because of the absence of any official enquiry the incident has passed into folklore, to join the Moloughney affair, the roughing up of Larry Stanley, the assault on Tommy Murphy, the Battle of New Ross, the destruction of the Antrim footballers by Kerry in 1946 and the "Tunnel of Hate" incident during the 1983 All-Ireland final.

But while the arguments raged in the pubs of Ireland

the clinching evidence of what really happened was available on film. The National Film Institute of Ireland made a film of that All-Ireland, and many others of course. As the camera moves away from Ring and Burke, to follow the play, the blow is recorded in the top right-hand corner of the screen. However, to study it properly the film must be run frame by frame. Is it really worth the effort?

Curiosity is not to be underestimated, and curiosity is increased by mystery which, in turn, is created by widely-differing versions of a relatively simple incident which thousands of GAA followers regard as an integral part of the folklore of the games. If that were not the case these episodes would have been long since forgotten.

Later that autumn I saw half that Cork team in action again in the first Cork County Final I ever attended. It was a very one-sided match in which Glen Rovers beat Sarsfields easily, but the huge crowd in the Athletic Grounds and the excitement of the Glen Rovers supporters afterwards, showed me clearly what hurling meant in Cork City — something I had not previously understood. There was also a big following there for soccer, a smaller one from a different class for rugby, with gaelic football more confined to the rural areas to the west than it is at present.

It was impossible to get away from the Ban. My daily work took me into secondary and technical schools and one situation in Cork City was a great source of amusement to me.

In the North Monastery the emphasis was on Irish and on gaelic games, particularly hurling. Looking back on it now I do not remember ever having seen a football around the place. Foreign games were regarded with horror. There was a tremendous air of dedication to causes in the school, including the causes of learning and passing examinations, but it was a cheerful air and I always looked forward to a visit and a chat with the pupils about their favourite topic — Cork hurling.

Down town, the same Christian Brothers ran Christian College which was, and still is, a rugby-playing institution.

142

Here the pupils spoke Irish haltingly and with a "refeened" accent; even the Brothers seemed different. How did this situation come about? I felt it would be embarrassing, if not actually indelicate, to ask a Brother in either school directly; it would be something akin to my Waterville gaffe.

One night, while having a nourishing bottle or two with that well-known past pupil of the North Monastery, Seán O Ríordáin, the subject was mentioned. Seán claimed to know of a meeting between a group of Cork businessmen and the Bishop of Cork, Dr Daniel Cohalan. These businessmen had come to the conclusion that while Presentation College was all very well in its way, and also a good rugby school, what their boys really needed was an education from the Jesuits. A small delegation went to see the Bishop and, after the usual small-talk, the spokesman came to the point.

"We were talking about Religious Orders in the club the other night, your Grace, and how terribly strange it was that the Jesuits never came to Cork . . . ."

Before he got any further the Bishop sniffed and said quickly, "I would regard that as a remarkable manifestation of the power of prayer."

That was the end of that but, according to Seán, the Bishop then asked the Christian Brothers to provide alternative education and suitable sporting and social activities for those who required them and everyone lived happily ever after.

The country was full of subtle differences and anomalies and there was plenty of time to observe them. Why was it, for instance, that at a time when it was almost impossible for a lay secondary teacher in any diocese in Ireland to get episcopal permission to open a secondary school, that west Limerick was full of such schools, with not a Christian Brother in sight between Adare and Charleville?

Most of my time was spent displaying my mobile selection of Irish books in schools, and sometimes in shops which we rented for short periods in certain towns, promoting the various papers and periodicals and An Club

Leabhar (The Irish Book Club), and making myself available to any organisation or event for which my services were requested from An Chomhdháil.

These requests were the bane of my life, and I soon found out that my mother's observations on how committees worked were very accurate. I also discovered how that committee horse ended up as a camel. The element of tug-of-war was very obvious. If the publishers of *Inniu* found out that I had spent a week in Kerry promoting An Club Leabhar, they demanded my services in Clare for a week to promote the paper in the schools.

During An Tóstal — an Ireland at Home Festival, organised by the Irish Tourist Board in the fifties, in an attempt to extend the tourist season at its coldest end — myself and Tomás Mac Gabhann provided an Irish ingredient in scores of cultural exhibitions, from one end of the country to the other. (More memorably, I was present at the official opening at the GPO when the Deputy Lord Mayor of Dublin concluded his speech by wishing our Tóstal visitors, "A hearty Slán Leat!")

Sometimes we were called back to Dublin to brief our employers, who were supposed to digest our ideas but who usually had their minds made up before they even heard us. The general disorganisation did not trouble me in the least in the early months, but when I became familiar with the territory, had scratched certain towns off my personal map forever, forged permanent bonds of friendship in strategic locations, and sorted out the good hotels from the dumps, these sudden switches of direction did not suit me at all.

During the summer months, for instance, I was directed to pay a visit to all the Irish Colleges, from Coláiste Charman in Gorey to Coláiste Chonnacht in An Spidéal, once during each three and a half week course. This was not only a piece of cake but it also enabled me to plot my travels with an eye to all the important hurling and football championship matches, and come back to Dublin for a fresh supply of books when the semi-final stages were reached.

It worked very well until Brian Mac Cafaid began to do favours for his old friends in the Gaelic League by offering me as a kind of cultural fire-eater for their annual feiseanna which were always held on Sundays.

I went to one for the experience and to learn, if possible, how to avoid this irritating impediment to my enjoyment of life in the future. It was held in a field near a technical school in south Tipperary and during the course of the day, which I spent staring at the four walls and ceiling of the room where my books were laid out for inspection and sale, thinking of what I was missing in various ways in other parts of the country, I failed to sell even one book.

People came to the door of the room all right, and even peered in like hungry hens at a kitchen door, only to withdraw again muttering, "Yerra, all t'auld books are in Irish", before moving off to the dancing platform. Towards evening, as the crowd were engrossed in the final stages of the dancing competitions, a young woman who looked as bored as I was feeling sailed into the room and walked around slowly, fingering the books absent-mindedly and ignoring me completely.

Soldiers in the First Irish-speaking Battalion had a phrase to describe the young women who paraded up and down the streets of the town in the evenings, talking animatedly and looking straight ahead when they passed the soldiers who manned Walsh's corner, at Eyre Square, and other recognised look-out posts: "Tá siad ag tróláil" (They have the trawl out). So before I even got the cigarettes out I was fairly certain I was lodged in the cod end of this young lady's trawl.

Things progressed slowly, as was customary at the time, but also very well. She knew I travelled around the country and wanted to know how she would set about getting a job in a hotel. I was an absolute mine of information.

Did she have any experience? She said she was actually being trained as a cook and housekeeper but her parents did not want her to leave home. But she found the place terribly boring. I agreed that it looked like the back of God-speed to me too. There was no social life at all. No congenial company either, that might shorten a dreary night for a fine girl like her? She was sure I said that to all the girls but it was true for me. Not alone were the fellows thick and ill-mannered but they were dreadfully rough, if I knew what she meant. This was more like it. Any minute now we could dispense with the code-book.

And indeed, that was the case, and just as I was beginning to forget the match in Limerick, the Castle Hotel in Galway, and everything else I had been missing a few minutes previously, and beginning to demonstrate how gentle and positively couth a knight of the road could be, the door opened suddenly and in walked the Irish teacher shouting, in high good humour, "Good news, Breandán, the Parish Priest would like to join An Club Leabhar."

Just as the thought struck me that this was surely a Blythian plot there came another roar from behind him: "Annie, you strap! What are you doing in here? Get up to the house this minute."

Among the things I learned in the next few minutes was that Parish Priests' housekeepers were not all middle-aged hairpins pickled in prudery. I also learned that the poor Irish teacher was even more committee-ridden than I was, without benefit of four wheels and a province and a half to move in, and that he would be very grateful if I got to hell out of the place and never came back.

That was an end to feiseanna, as far as I was concerned, but to keep my supervisor at bay I was careful to organise totally non-existent cultural activities, in the vicinity of my own true interests, every weekend during the summer. These usually took the form of meetings with enthusiasts who were engaged in experimental projects. As most of the supervisor's Sundays were spent fishing with the Bishop of Dromore and other dignitaries of the church, he did not have time to chase me . . . yet.

But before that particular pursuit began in earnest

something completely new and unexpected entered the language revival movement. I was sitting in the bar of the Imperial Hotel in Limerick, having a drink with Joe Keohane, when I was told that the secretary of An Chomhdháil, Donncha O Laoire, wanted to talk to me on the telephone. As if I were conditioning myself for the day of reckoning, my heart always missed a beat when I heard the office was looking for me, even when I had nothing in particular to worry about.

Donncha sounded very excited by the news he had for me. A football pool called Gael Linn had just been established, and it was going to be run on gaelic games with the aim of raising money to promote Irish in various ways. I was being seconded to Gael Linn for a period, to distribute books to promoters who would collect the shilling a week entry fee, and was to return to Dublin immediately to be briefed by Dónal O Móráin, whose idea Gael Linn was, and who was anxious to get as many promoters as possible working as soon as possible. I had had only a little contact with Dónal O Móráin at that point but the last part of the message seemed to be in character. I went back to Joe Keohane and we discussed the implications of the new departure.

9

Two days later I was back in the Imperial Hotel with a load of pool cards and publicity material. Following Joe Keohane's advice I had chosen an area where the GAA was strong, where I was reasonably well-known and where he could provide me with contacts: West Limerick and North Kerry. I was tempted to choose Galway but one of my "moles" in the office had informed me that my frequent visits to that town were already the subject of comment. It seemed to some that even a simple journey from Dublin to Bray had to take in Galway.

The Imperial Hotel — now, sadly, but a memory — was a great meeting-place for GAA followers and players. It was run by Mrs Sadlier, whose daughter Peggy was married to Joe Keohane who was stationed in Limerick at the time. I happened on the hotel when sent to Limerick to organise an exhibition of books and a series of lectures on writing in Irish in the City Library. For the remainder of my time on the road it was my home from home whenever my work took me to that region. Mrs Sadlier ran a tight ship and when she said "Go" you went. In my mind's eye I can still see her coming into the bar and hear her declare: "You're not having a pint, Breandán. You're going up to the dining-room this minute and having your tea."

Among the permanent guests were two brothers who were in the building business, Dinny and Seán Lanigan. Dinny won All-Irelands with Limerick in 1918 and 1921 and was a dedicated follower of hurling. It was he who first aroused my curiosity about Michael Cusack and why it was that the GAA seemed so reluctant to honour its founder by introducing him to people like myself who knew little or nothing about him. All Dinny Lanigan said was, "Cusack was a difficult man", and went on to talk of other things. But although I did little to increase my knowledge for many years the seeds of curiosity were sown.

One night, after an evening challenge match between Limerick and Kilkenny on an Ascension Thursday, there was a great gathering of old hurlers in the bar of the Imperial and Dinny Lanigan made one of his rare appearances in that part of the house. For me, it was an occasion to remember forever, and one when the mouth was kept closed and the ears wide open.

Mick Mackey was there and Jim Langton, as well as Paddy Grace, Jimmy O'Connell (who was the goalkeeper in the 1940 final) and many others whose names I cannot recollect for, naturally enough, the stars were the centre of my attention. What struck me then, and what I remember now — thirty years later — was the laughter and the endless stories of humorous incidents, on and off the field, even in All-Ireland Finals. Jimmy O'Connell, for instance, reminded Mick Mackey of the first shot he fired at him in the 1940 All-Ireland, which he saved and cleared, but Mackey kept running in and as he turned at the edge of the square, shouted, "You're in good form but you won't smell the next one." Mick Mackey pleaded a defective memory.

The occasion reminded me of a family reunion without any of the tensions which very often simmer under the veneer of politeness at some of these gatherings. Football and hurling create a national family but hurling, being a far more skilful game embracing a variety of regional styles (for all that it is the minority sport), seems to sharpen the appreciation of skills for their own sake and outside of regional preferences. This may not be as true of many supporters as it is of the players. Supporters are generally more fanatical and blinkered by county allegiances and are not as detached or as knowledgeable as the best players are.

There were many other such nights in the Imperial but I do not remember them as clearly as that first one. But I was always struck by the contrast between the relaxed, humorous atmosphere of these gatherings and the dour and forbidding aspect of the GAA's public face. It was very like the difference between a good night in a Gaeltacht pub and one of the self-conscious socials Irish-speakers in Dublin organised from time to time. They too were supposed to be enjoyable but it was very constipated fun, as far as I was concerned.

It was from a priest who was with the Kilkenny team that Ascension Thursday night that I heard a story concerning two facets of the games which have now all but disappeared: the over-age minors and the planned invasion of the pitch as a means of forcing a replay.

It concerned another priest in a part of North Kilkenny where hurling was not as strong at the time as it was in the rest of the county. He was a dedicated apostle of hurling and decided to build a team of youngsters and take them up from grade to grade. After a lot of hard work and some set-backs, they reached the county minor final in which they met a team from the deep south.

When the teams took to the field the priest realised that a march had been stolen on them. Their opponents had a spine of muscular and hairy young men through their team, from full back to full forward. Caps pulled well down over their eyes they proceeded to hurl his young charges off the field as if they were so many flies on fresh cowdung. At half-time the game was already lost on the score-board but the priest's fury had turned to more calculating anger and he laid a trap for his unscrupulous opponents.

There was but one big, strong player on his team, the full back, and he was switched to mid-field with an instruction to start a fight at the first opportunity. The others were to rush to the scene as would the priest and all the supporters he had gathered on the sideline nearby. They would then refuse to leave the field, there would be a hearing at the County Board and he would sort out the matter of the over-age players before they vanished into thin air with the cup and medals.

The player was strong and willing but he was not the brightest and as the game progressed with no sign of the planned brawl the priest began to wonder what had gone wrong. Then, as the player and his opponent raced towards the sideline, where the priest and his assault party were massed, after a ball that beat them both to the line, the player shouted at the top of his voice, "Is it time to start creeling them now, Father?"

As I started to "creel" the people of West Limerick and North Kerry with Gael Linn publicity I was reminded of the Galway saying, which can be roughly translated thus: "The people of Ardrahan are as one, but they do not necessarily keep their money in a communal pocket." The ordinary citizens were very interested and enthusiastic about the new venture and its motives and there was no difficulty in getting promoters and collectors.

But while GAA members, players and followers of the games were as enthusiastic as one would expect them to be, I became aware of a definite reserve when I encountered some of the more senior officials. The higher up the hierarchical ladder I went the more this reserve resembled suspicion, if not antagonism.

One old player would not have anything to do with it unless I could guarantee that a percentage of Gael Linn's takings would go towards the GAA Accident Fund. He was a blunt man and I heard that even during his playing days he had to be approached with a high degree of circumspection.

A contemporary, who welcomed me warmly, laughed when I told him the story. He remembered being in a car that was collecting players for a Railway Cup semi-final against Connacht one February and the conversation about the general state of unfitness got more intense as the car filled up. My man who was concerned about the

Accident Fund was the last man to be picked up from the bottom of the road that led to his farm. He sat in and said nothing. After a short silence someone said to him: "I suppose you're killed after the ploughing?" to which he replied, "I never felt better but the two horses are shagged."

As I was doing my best to place as many books as I could, and get as many shillings as possible rattling off to Dublin, I did not have the time to seek reasons for my instinctive feeling that all was not really well between Gael Linn and the GAA. As well as feeling Brian Mac Cafaid's breath on the back of my neck I now felt Dónal Ó Móráin's gimlet eyes boring a hole through it. However, all you need in such a situation is to meet one person who likes to be in a position to tell you something that you do not know: particularly if it is something that is bound to upset you. Before my term of secondment was over I met such a man.

He informed me that Croke Park, which in those days really meant Paddy O'Keefe, the General Secretary of the GAA, was not all that happy about Gael Linn. Croke Park had heard that this pool was actually going to be run on soccer until second, and wiser, thoughts prevailed. Having spent some weeks in Kerry I replied innocently that I found all that very strange for did not the world and his wife know that Paddy O'Keefe's side-kick, Seán Ó Síocháin, was one of the trustees of Gael Linn. The man said that indeed it was the case but that it was another day's work. Many dedicated Gaels, he said, wondered how the GAA was going to benefit by all this.

Surely, said I, the GAA is delighted to see the Language (you said it with a capital letter in rarefied English-speaking company) benefit in this way and wouldn't the games be played anyway? That indeed was the case but the GAA had its own priorities and would have to keep them uppermost in its thoughts at all times. I kept this conversation to myself and then pressing personal problems sent it out of my mind until later tensions, which enter into my story, helped to bring it back to mind.

I had better make it clear that at this stage I had had just about a bellyful of a certain type of Gael: pronounced as the English word "Gale" which was a corruption of the other word but singularly appropriate as most of them were as full of wind as Joyce's "tanyard cat". I had also better make it clear, now that the Gael is a vanishing species, that there were various types of Gael.

Some were first and foremost Irish speakers and worked ceaselessly for its revival and some of these despised the GAA for being hypocritical in its attitude to the language. Then there was the Gael who spoke Irish but devoted most of his attention to sustaining the GAA. There were Gaels who were in favour of the revival of Irish, who did not speak a word of it but were staunch supporters of the GAA. There were also Gaels who saw the language as an unnecessary complication in the straightforward business of promoting the games and, although they could take a few ritualistic words of it (or leave it alone for that matter) it was rather like a speck of dirt in the sporting eye. And there were Gaels who thought the language revival was plain daft, but most of these only gave voice to their true sentiments privately and after a feed of drink.

Finally, there was the Gael who gave me the horrors without benefit of drink. To qualify for this particular grade of Gaeldom the title-bearer did not have to play football or hurling, go to a match, sing a ballad, dance a jig or speak Irish. He merely had to approve of these activities. Far more necessary to his code was aggressive opposition to those who disagreed with his outlook. These unfortunates, outside this new version of the Pale, were insulted at every opportunity and usually referred to as "enemies of Gaeldom who have broken faith with the past."

Nobody knows who coined the term Gael. According to Fr Mark Tierney it was first used in connection with members of the GAA who marched in uniform in 1887. As far as I was concerned, after a year and a bit of too close acquaintance, it had lingered in its contemporary sense long enough to outlive its uselessness.

The high point in my experience of the Gael was reached in an Ennis hotel one wet night at a time when I was off the drink and had already seen the film in the Gaiety Cinema. I was reading a book when my ear homed in on a meeting in the adjoining room which was being conducted in Irish. It was a committee of the Gaelic League planning the St Patrick's Day activities. It was terribly boring and the book was ahead by a point or two when a row started. It was a low-key row at first but it got better rapidly and I then found that I could identify three or four of the participants by their voices.

The row was about the céilí which was once the great annual fund-raising occasion until it was decided, two years previously, that the Clare Set was a Foreign Dance ("Damhsa Gallda" was the term used) and banned. Instead of making money they had a slight deficit the previous year and some of the younger members of the committee wanted the suspension on the Clare Set lifted forthwith.

The chairman, an elderly Christian Brother, led the counter-attack. It was a well-known fact that the proper name for the Clare Set was the Caledonian Set and where did these whipper-snappers think that came from, he asked in a typical Christian Brother's rising cadence? He was backed up by a vocational teacher who went into a rage about the absence of the accepted steps of official Irish dancing and the *sliding* and the *battering*. He worked himself up into a fury.

To cut this incredible story short it was then discovered that nowhere was it clearly specified that the offending dance was a foreign one, like a waltz or a fox-trot. This led to further argument until someone proposed that a set be danced in another room (presumably to protect the purity of the committee-room), that the committee would observe it and a vote would then be taken on whether or not it was a native or a foreign dance. This was done, to the huge amusement of the hotel staff who were recruited for this curious demonstration, and to no surprise at all the ban was confirmed by the vote. One member of the committee could not stomach it. Telling the Christian Brother, the vocational teacher and some of the others that they ought to be in the local looney bin, he resigned and went off, presumably to drink himself sane.

Some years later I became briefly involved in a discussion on what a Gael — even a True Gael — actually was. Brendan Behan summoned me from my place of work to render some assistance in a pub in Baggot Street. He was drinking with a little man called "Mouse" Donegan who was making heavy demands on Brendan's financial resources, as he had no money himself, having been released from Mountjoy that morning after a three-month spell for being caught in the pursuit of his profession as a cat-burglar.

When I arrived, Brendan was having an argument with another customer, an ex-President of the Gaelic League called Diarmuid Mac Fhionnlaoich, on the subject of Gaels and their beliefs. Brendan was in rare form for leg-pulling and had convinced Diarmuid that he was in deadly earnest as he denigrated all aspects of the Irish revival and mocked the GAA.

"You are certainly not a True Gael," said Diarmuid, as he left for the toilet in bad temper.

"Neither are you," said Brendan, which was the point he had been heading for all the time. "A True Gael is a loaf of bread that's baked by O'Rourke below in Store Street" (There was, at the time, indeed such a loaf on sale).

This really annoyed Diarmuid and as he disappeared Brendan said to me: "I hope he doesn't take it too seriously" and by way of explanation to "Mouse", who seemed to have taken his own share of ribbing earlier, "He's the son of a really great man called 'Cú Uladh', if you ever heard of him?"

"Mouse" decided he had had enough and, putting on his best sneer, replied, "Didn't I know him well. Many's the few bob I won on him above in Harold's Cross."

"Watch yourself, you little gobshite, if you want to keep drinking in this company," said Brendan angrily and changed the subject.

My own parting with An Chomhdháil was preceded by a kind of death-wish which took the form of outrageous and reckless behaviour and which would have terminated my employment much earlier had not Tomás Mac Gabhann, in particular, and good friends and some very considerate members of the Gárda Síochána in Galway not come to my assistance in various hours of need.

Like my leaving of UCG, it was only when the job was gone and I was again back in Inis Mór with one arm as long as the other, as they say, that the serious side of the situation began to dawn on me. My final brush with the law took place near Dublin and before the law could lay its hands on me I fled across country and lay low for a few days, feeling instinctively that An Chomhdháil would smooth things over, if that were possible, to keep its good name out of the papers — even if that meant applying a poultice of green medication to the injured party's bruised dignity. My instinct was accurate and I then returned to Dublin to face the music.

Partly because my work, when I applied myself to it, was satisfactory and partly because of my comparative youth, the board was inclined to deal leniently with me at first. After all it was my first offence. In like a flash came my minder with a correction: the first offence that had come to their notice. Then, I was told later, skeleton after skeleton tumbled out of my closet until the floor of the office was covered. Brian had spent a productive two days on the phone and made up for lost time. In the end I was lucky that good friends on the board persuaded the others to give me the option of resigning. As if that were not punishment enough I happened to meet Máirtín Ó Cadhain, who was engaged in violent disputation with de Blaghd and An Chomhdháil at the time, who berated me for having returned the van. I should have headed for

Cleggan Pier, he said, and backed the whole lot into the sea. The way my luck had run out I would have probably forgotten to get out of the cab in time and, like most Aran Islanders of my generation, I cannot swim.

For good or ill, my next job, after an uneasy few months in Aran, led directly to my present way of life. Seán Ó hÉigeartaigh it was who rescued me and appointed me editor of his publishing company, Sáirséal agus Dill, although his financial resources were stretched to the limit at the time. It was more than a job for after a short time I felt like one of the family. His influence and that of his wife Bríd helped to exorcise most of the malign spirits that possessed me far too frequently at the time.

As hilarious coincidence would have it, the first manuscript I was given to edit was of Earnán de Blaghd's *Briseadh na Teorann* (The Breaking of the Border) in which he argued that the Northern Protestants demanded partition because they regarded the demand for a United Ireland as a religious and not a nationalistic goal. This was because the Irish Catholics had turned their backs on the Irish language and traditions, and re-unification would have to be preceded by a cultural revival through which a significant number of Northern Protestants would be convinced that something more than a mere Catholic Republic was planned for them.

One sentence of roughly 150 words seemed to call for my attention and without altering what sense I could get out of it one iota, I converted it into three tidy sentences of about thirty words each. When the edited typescript was returned to Earnán he called Seán and said that there was a slight difference between editing and butchering and would I please leave his prose style alone. I, in turn, protested to Seán that all I wanted to do was to point out to Earnán, in a polite way, that he was using language with the sensitivity of a washerwoman beetling a batch of blankets.

Seán looked at me quizzically as if to say "Are you really sure your motives are as disinterested as you say they are?" and Earnán had his way. Seán was probably right in feeling that the temptation to put my boot into my enemy had been a factor in my re-writing but I was cheered by the three-page glossary which was considered necessary as a key to the text. It included the term "pobal-ghuthrú plaincéadach" which sounds like a baby puking up its feed and which I will not spoil for you with a translation.

But in many ways Earnán was ahead of his time and the book contains many interesting suggestions. This passage concerns the GAA's role in crossing the religious divide in Northern Ireland (my translation):

Sporting and cultural bodies should shape their policies to help end the political and religious division and eventually the border. The GAA, for instance, should be very careful not to behave in the Six Counties as an organisation for Catholics only. Without abandoning any of its nationalism or gaelicism, the GAA should try to induce thousands of Protestants to watch their games and eventually play them. Therefore, Catholic hymns should neither be played nor sung before or after football or hurling matches, except on very special occasions. The national anthem (Amhrán na bhFiann) should not be played on such occasions in the Six Counties, nor should the major games be played on Sundays. It is not that I wish to force Protestant Sabbatarianism on Catholics; however, it is certain that if the GAA's principal matches in the North are not played on Saturdays, for some years to come, that organisation will be unable to do anything to bring about a united Ireland and anything its leaders say about ending partition will be fruitless talk. However, if the above suggestion were adopted as part of a national anti-partition policy, I have no doubt but that the GAA and its games would soon have the support of throngs of Protestants and another wall between Nationalist Catholics and Unionist Protestants would be demolished.

Earnán's message fell on deaf ears at the time for the book appeared just as the IRA campaign on the Border commenced. Seán Ó hEigeartaigh was approached by various people who wanted publication postponed because of Earnán's strictures on the IRA. Seán would not hear of it, no more than he would agree some years later to delete material from Mainchín Seoighe's biography, "Maraíodh Seán Sabhat Aréir" (Seán South was killed last night), which the Department of Education which controlled the grants that were paid to Irish publishers found offensive. Seán was a born publisher although all his other working life was spent as a senior civil servant in the Department of Finance.

Strangely enough, when one considers how bitterness and spite tend to grow deeper with time in Ireland, my own relationship with Earnán de Blaghd became quite cordial over the years. Indeed, I later had reason to be very grateful to him when I had my most shattering experience as a television presenter.

It was on *Féach* and the programme was a live one on the rapidly-developing Northern situation, and the effect it was likely to have on this state. We had Ruairí Ó Brádaigh of Provisional Sinn Féin, Tomás Mac Giolla of Official Sinn Féin, Professor Ruairí Ó hAnluain of UCD and Earnán de Blaghd.

Just a few hours before going on air someone in RTE decided that the Provisional Sinn Féin were not acceptable and the programme went on without Ruairí Ó Brádaigh, who mounted a protest picket outside with a group of supporters. The programme had hardly begun when Tomás Mac Giolla read a statement deploring the ban on Ó Brádaigh and announcing his own immediate departure from the programme in protest. He walked out and then there were two . . . .

While this was going on Earnán sat there drumming on the table with his fingers and looking very impatient. Ruairí Ó hAnluain looked to be even more nervous than I was but we had over twenty minutes to fill and much as

I felt like following Tomás Mac Giolla and going to the Merrion Inn for a drink I had to carry on. Then Earnán opened up. This was clearly the moment he had been waiting for. He had the ball, the field lay wide open before him and off he went on a solo run, with hardly a prompt from me, through all his pet theories and aversions, leaving the professor and myself with very little to do.

Afterwards, in the hospitality room, the programme researcher, Póilín Ní Chiaráin, introduced Earnán to Ruairí Ó Brádaigh who had come in to make a phone-call. The conversation, which was in Irish, of course, went something like this.

"Do you know Ruairí Ó Brádaigh, Earnán?"

"Ah, yes. You're the one who walked out."

(Not at any distance would even a half-blind man confuse the rotund Ó Brádaigh with the gaunt Mac Giolla).

"No, I'm the one they wouldn't let in."

"Ach, well, it's all the same really, you're all pure daft anyway."

Truth to tell I was not a very good editor and I was an even worse proof-reader. Only when we published a series of text-books in Irish for secondary schools did my past experience on the road benefit Sáirséal agus Dill and I got a lot of orders. But the road had decided to reject me. In my rush to get to Longford from Carrick-on-Shannon, before the schools broke for lunch, I went over a wall near Rooskey and wrote off Seán's beautiful Humber Super Snipe. That was my last journey as a salesman.

I had seen enough of the country to be going on with and little by little the appeal of Dublin grew stronger. It was Seán who suggested that journalism and broadcasting might prove more congenial to my taste and talents than anything I had tried my hand at so far.

To encourage me, he proposed that I take over from him the short talks in Irish which then preceded the rugby internationals on Radio Éireann. He was very interested in rugby and was chosen to give these preliminary talks when

Radio Éireann decided to introduce some Irish into their coverage of sports other than gaelic football and hurling. Niall Tóibín and Mícheál Ó Reachtara handled soccer and racing. This was something I enjoyed very much and, later, when television came, I spent some years commenting on games during the international season.

As well as being enjoyable, it was also a challenge to find simple forms of speech to describe an activity which was neither discussed nor written about in Irish to any great extent. My interpolations sounded quaint to some and drove one particular resident of the Greystones area to ring up and register a protest as soon as ever I opened my mouth during a match. But I was surprised by the number of followers of the game who would come to me in bars, in various parts of the country, to tell me that they agreed with some comment of mine or that I had been talking through my hat.

The practice was abandoned when the RFU began to play two international matches on the same Saturday and BBC Northern Ireland took the RTE commentary on the match in which Ireland was engaged. Someone decided that it would not be right or proper to inflict my few comments in Irish on Northern ears. Personally, I did not mind being dropped as my interests had by then taken another turn. And indeed it was a salutary lesson in how one national minority could expect to be treated in a United Ireland — or, indeed, in any kind of Ireland.

My most vivid memory from this period is of the match in Cardiff Arms Park when Brian Price of Wales laid out Noel Murphy with a haymaker, right under the referee's nose and in front of the box where Prince Charles was seated. He was paying his first visit to the Park in his capacity as Prince of Wales and it seems that the referee did not want to spoil his day by sending a player to the line. But as I watched the Irish players gesticulating and wondering what to do, and poor Murphy stretched on the ground, I said to myself, "Jesus, there are the hard men! Now, if you were the Crusheen, Rathnew or Buffers

Alley hurlers you would hurl the jock-straps off those Welsh hoors all the way to Holyhead." Which only goes to show that in times of stress we all revert to type. But I was careful not to express these sentiments on the air.

And while I was still engaged in this activity, I was invited to contribute an article in Irish to the GAA annual, which I gladly did. The Ban was still on the statute books at the time and at a Central Council meeting, after publication of the annual, a Longford delegate complained that there was not a single mention, pictorial or otherwise, of Longford in the magazine. Someone murmured something about considerations of space to which he replied, hopping the annual off the floor as he spoke, "Yes, but you found room for a bloody rugby commentator."

As far as I am aware that was my last brush with that particular species of Gael . . . and I was not even there to enjoy it.

10

One entered journalism in those days through the door of a shop that was wide open. Most journalists on the Dublin dailies and Sunday papers arrived from the provincial press, the majority of them from the west and north of Ireland. Others, particularly the sub-editors and feature writers, came into the trade from other occupations and there was a great shifting shoal of casual and freelance practitioners moving around the town.

Journalism was not a particularly well-paid job in the fifties, nor was it really regarded as one of the respectable professions, and one of the first pieces of advice I got when I joined the *Irish Press*, from one of the few women journalists in the place, was never to borrow money from a printer. She maintained that printers despised journalists for not being craftsmen like themselves.

Indeed, a degree of tension did exist. This was the age of hot metal and the printer had to serve a long apprenticeship. On one occasion I heard a printer tell a journalist friend of mine, who had addressed him with coarse familiarity, to watch his tongue when speaking to a craftsman.

The journalist, whose tongue was as facile as his pen, replied that he saw nothing in the craft of printing, as practised by this particular individual, that a fairly intelligent fifteen year old could not be taught in six months in a technical school. Grave exception was taken to this insult to the craft.

After a period as a freelance jack-of-all-trades around

the town, I was eventually appointed Irish Editor of Irish Press Newspapers and was to begin my duties in the first week in January 1957. It was a pleasure to go home for Christmas bearing good news and able to give a definite answer to those who asked me if I was leaving at any particular time. My father, who greatly approved of this departure, was as happy as I was myself but my mother was not terribly impressed.

In her individualistic view, journalism was not really a profession at all, rather a terrestrial form of piracy on the high seas. The few practitioners of the trade she had encountered she disliked, finding them to be "full of vice and hideousness" — not altogether as bad as commercial travellers but clearly belonging in the same league.

Like Comrade Lenin, she seemed to define a journalist as one who had failed in his chosen profession and I was certainly in no position to contradict her. But sensing that I had become hopelessly addicted to the piratical life, my mother suggested that perhaps I should take up sports journalism. It seemed to offer a healthier ambience. She knew very little about sport but in her mind it was associated with cleanliness, fresh air, people who did not smoke or drink and who were not mixed up in politics.

When I returned to Burgh Quay, two days late, I found the editor of the *Irish Press*, Jim McGuinness, worried in case I had become involved in the IRA campaign on the Border which was then at its height. Indeed, I well remember hearing the first report of the Brookeborough raid on the radio in Aran. When it said that one of the two dead men was believed to be from Limerick, my sister Máirín, who was a teacher in Limerick at the time, and myself, immediately said, "Poor Seán South."

My reasons for not being in the IRA at that time need not detain us here, but they do not necessarily reflect any great credit on me, much as I would like to claim it — not having much in the line of a national record, fashionable or otherwise. However, Jim McGuinness who was in the IRA in London during the bombing campaign in 1939 and was afterwards interned in the Curragh, was relieved to find that a mere storm in Galway Bay was responsible for my late return.

I took to the *Irish Press* like a seagull to flying and the air of barely-controlled lunacy that existed there at the time was just what I needed, as well as the constant discipline of the deadline that had to be met.

I moved into a small hotel near the junction of Talbot Street and Gardiner Street, a few minutes walk from the office, and settled down to learn the trade. In time I also branched out into a few others but there have been very few days since January 1957 when I have not written something. I find that activity just as exciting, and much more challenging, now as I did in those early weeks when I began my first column in the *Sunday Press*.

The *Irish Press* could easily hijack the remainder of this entertainment. It was easily the most colourful place I ever worked in as well as being a continuation of my interrupted education. The place was full of people who had already made their names in various journalistic and writing activities, as well as a batch of hungry young reporters who were about to follow them. But although this is an entertainment it does have a certain purpose and, as Christy Ring is supposed to have said, when asked to give advice to aspiring hurlers, "Always keep your eye on the ball, even when the referee has it."

One of the first members of the staff I got to know was Pádraig Puirséal — Paddy as we called him — who had left the sport temporarily and was looking after the Features Department, under the roof where the Irish Editor was based: proof-readers who had to climb up the stairs with death notices and advertisements in Irish, for correction, irreverently referred to it as "The Erse-Hole".

Paddy was most welcoming, as indeed were all the senior members of the staff without exception, but when he found out that I had a great interest in what was to him a passion, we got on even better. It is a great help, when meeting any writer for the first time, to be able to say that you have read his books. My father had Paddy's four novels at home and I remarked to him, as others have done, before and since, on how the national addiction to sport in general and gaelic games in particular, was reflected in contemporary writing. Even in his own books hurling is fleetingly glimpsed in *Hanrahan's Daughter*.

During this conversation I found out that coverage of gaelic games in the national newspapers (with one glaring exception), on the scale to which I was accustomed, was of somewhat recent origin. This came as a shock to me, being aware of the GAA's almost immediate mass appeal. So I went through the bound copies of the daily papers in the National Library and in our own library in Burgh Quay. Reading through the actual newspapers is a pleasure in itself and I regard the advent of microfilm, despite its obvious advantages, as an abomination. What follows is a summary of what I learned about how the GAA broke into the daily papers.

The 1931 All-Ireland hurling final was probably the most significant in the history of the GAA. Not only did the first contest and the two replays attract an attendance of 92,000 (and earn £8,000 for the Central Council), but the mounting interest generated tremendous publicity and helped to create one of the great traditions of hurling.

A woman reporter from the *Irish Independent*, writing about the second replay, when Cork eventually overcame Kilkenny, probably summed up the feelings of the newcomers to Croke Park:

When once the ball was in, the hurlers were flashes of lightning rather than men. Their speed for their size was an eye-opener. The game was so swift throughout that one's eye was not quick enough to follow it: the speed was simply terrific, the career of the players and the ball from one end of the pitch to the other catapultic. Thus must the Fianna have proven themselves in their mighty tests on the plains of Ireland, and the ancient Greeks, both away back in the beginning of time. There is nothing to be found anywhere in the world like it. We have got to make it the game of all others in this country.

The final sentence must have caused eyebrows to raise in Croke Park, for I noticed that the GAA authorities were beginning to rightly complain, at this very time, of the lack of interest in their games shown by the Dublin newspapers.

The authorities were particularly worried by poor attendances at hurling finals. The attendances at the finals between 1927 and 1930, in rounded figures, were: 24,000; 15,000; 14,000; and 22,000. It was felt that better press coverage would help to swell the attendances and the association's coffers. Two events combined to grant the GAA its wish: two great teams playing classical hurling, and the advent of a new daily paper, the *Irish Press*.

Cork and Kilkenny had not met in an All-Ireland since 1912, but those with a deep knowledge of hurling knew that the elements for a great match existed, as "Pato" wrote in his miniscule "Gaelic Ghetto" in the *Irish Times*, before the first meeting: "Critics have written up Cork and Kilkenny as being on the same plane of skill. They play scientific hurling as opposed to the dare-devil rushing tactics of Tipperary, Galway, Limerick and Clare."

There were stars in plenty on both sides, men whose names are still household words in their native counties and beyond. There was Lory (Lorenzo) Meagher of Kilkenny, one of the greatest players of all time in the opinion of those who were lucky enough to have seen him play. Then there were Eudie Coughlan, Dinny Barry Murphy, Jim Hurley (I noticed that the medal he won in 1931 was worn on his watch-chain by his grandson when he was called to the Bar in 1984) and the Ahearnes of Cork, Dermody, the Kilkenny goalkeeper, Paddy Phelan, the Larkins and Matt Power: one could say that all thirty players were first-class hurlers.

The first meeting was generally described as the best

All-Ireland for a decade, and a draw the most fitting result. It was a most dramatic draw with Eudie Coughlan, the Cork captain, scoring the equalising point while on his knees, as the referee was putting the whistle in his mouth to blow full time.

The newspapers responded by giving the replay more advance coverage than had been given to any All-Ireland final in the past. I would say that this was partly, at least, a response to the fact that the *Irish Press* gave a full page preview to the first match.

It is one of the legends of Burgh Quay that when the Sports Editor, Joe Sherwood from Workington, in Cumbria, handed the lay-out of the page to the compositor, it was handed back with the instruction that, whatever about alphabetical order, the pictures of the Kilkenny team were to go on top of the page, and the Cork players at the bottom — the compositor being a strong supporter of the Kilkenny team. Joe Sherwood vouched for the accuracy of the story and certainly that is how they appeared.

For the replay the *Irish Independent* ran a forecast competition with large cash prizes and the *Irish Press* ran its first "training camp special" over four days with surprisingly-detailed pen-pictures of the players. The *Irish Times* gave "Pato" an extra few inches, but kept its sporting sights firmly fixed on hockey, rugby and golf.

The replay, on October 11th, was even better than the first match and it was decided not to play extra time, as the rule ordained, because of the exhausted state of the players. Dermody, the Kilkenny goalie, was the man of the match and again, Cork just snatched the vital score inside the last minute of play. Paddy Delea, the full forward, was the saviour on this occasion. Unfortunately for Kilkenny Lory Meagher suffered two broken ribs and was considered doubtful for the next encounter.

This time the newspapers spread themselves on the game. The *Irish Press* printed a large photograph on the top of the front page. It showed something which was to become, unfortunately in my view, "part and parcel of every Gaelic occasion" (to coin a phrase) for years to come. It showed the Cork captain kneeling to kiss the ring of Archbishop Harty of Cashel.

Not to be outdone, "Pato" dragged a General and a brace of Bishops into his report in the *Irish Times*: "I met General O'Duffy, Archbishop Hayden, Archbishop Harty and Dr Broderick after the game. They said they never saw a faster, cleaner and more inspiring struggle. I could not help agreeing, for it was a severe game throughout, without serious fouls at any stage, and play swayed with pulsating interest from end to end."

The second replay was played on a heavier sod, on All Saints Day, and Cork won by 5-8 to 3-4. According to the *Irish Independent* report, "They were the steady war-worn championship fighters, who played themselves out to the bitter end, whilst Kilkenny played in flashes."

It was a victory marred by the absence of Lory Meagher, for no one could say what his presence might have meant to Kilkenny. Towards the end of the game, when a Kilkenny player was being substituted, the Kilkenny supporters began to chant "Lory; Lory." Puirséal in his book *The GAA in its Time* describes Lory's presence at the game as he remembered it: "I can still see him in my mind's eye as I saw him then, in his best suit, hunched and bowed on the touchline seat, white-knuckled hands clasped tightly on a hurley, tears running down his cheeks because he could not answer his county's urgent call."

The Central Council presented all the players who took part in those epic games with gold watches, as a special gesture. The crowds who came to see them returned to Croke Park in increasing numbers: the 1932 All-Ireland drew 34,000 and 45,000 came to watch Kilkenny play Limerick in 1933. The moral of that is as valid today as it was then, for those who fail to realise that the GAA's greatest asset is the healthy state of hurling and football.

It is also revealing to add that by the time Cork and Kilkenny met again in a final, relations between the GAA and the newspapers had again turned sour. Ever eager to seek an enemy to savage, outside the ivory gates, the GAA declared war on the Dublin newspapers in 1938. Seán McCarthy, a Fianna Fáil TD from Cork and a member of the Central Council, threatened to withhold advertisements from the papers unless they improved their coverage of gaelic games.

It was to be a phoney war but before it petered out, the *Irish Press* quoted figures in its own defence, showing that since its foundation the coverage given by its main rival, the *Irish Independent*, to gaelic games had increased ten-fold!

The *Irish Times*, I noticed, kept its nose disdainfully distant from this vulgar Celtic squabble. By 1939 it had decided to publish photographs of the teams taking part in the All-Irelands and when Kilkenny met Cork in 1946, a small paragraph giving the result and the attendance appeared on the front page for the first time.

It took a Waterford hurler called Donal Foley to change all that and show the paper that gaelic games are both important and commercially beneficial. But that in turn did not mean that certain entrenched attitudes to the paper changed. Some years ago, I was very pleased to be given one of the GAA's Mac Con Midhe Awards for a piece I had published about memories of All-Irelands I had seen as a boy. At the reception, I was congratulated by one of the best-known GAA county secretaries in the country who asked me where the piece had appeared, as he could not remember having read it. I told him that it had appeared in the *Irish Times* on the Saturday before the All-Hurling final the previous year.

"That explains it," he said, "I never read that paper", in a tone similar to the one I would use if talking about the *Sun*.

It must have been this prolonged browse through the sports pages that aroused my interest in the peculiar style adopted by most writers when reporting and discussing gaelic games. I was always interested in sports writing, and particularly in American writing on the subject. I had read Hemingway, Damon Runyon, Ring Lardner, A.J. Liebling and others, as well as the great English writer on cricket and music, Neville Cardus. But for whatever reason I never paid any attention to either the style or the linguistic idiosyncrasies of the writers on gaelic games. The only piece of writing on the subject that remained in my memory was a piece on the front page of the *Irish Press*: a colour story, as these descriptive pieces are called, on a match between Cavan and Cork, by Benedict Kiely.

Ben was Literary Editor and film critic of the paper and I was lucky enough to share an office with him for most of my six years in the place. They were great years too, and apart from becoming close friends it was from him I learned most of what I know about the craft of journalism and how to organise one's work. At a time of great purges in the paper there was a story going the rounds that the management often wanted to get rid of us but could never manage to find either of us at the right time.

Ben told a story about that particular match. Himself and Séamus de Faoite, the short story writer from Killarney, were sent there together to give an Ulster and a Munster view of the action. Séamus, who worked as a subeditor, was probably the most dedicated Kerry supporter that I ever met. He took Kerry football very seriously indeed, as I found out on the night that the incredible news came that Waterford footballers had beaten Kerry in the first round of the Munster championship. As I was going up the stairs Séamus came down towards me and I should have known by the look on his face that he was best left alone, but I had to crack my feeble joke: "I hear your hurlers took a hammering today." Fortunately, I was always very fast off my mark and could lead even good runners over the first fifteen yards. I was also lucky that we were friends and that he abandoned the chase at the first bend of the staircase.

In the game that he covered with Ben he transferred most of his Kerry bias to the next best thing who had to be good to have beaten Kerry anyway. Cavan won by a small margin and Big Peter Donohoe, the great Cavan full-forward and a friend of Ben's, was the top scorer. On the way back to the office Séamus was smouldering and Ben thought it better to discuss anything and everything but the match. But there is a limit to this kind of avoidance of a delicate subject and when they stopped for a drink, Ben made the first move by stating what he considered to be an obvious and indisputable fact: "Big Peter played well, I thought." Séamus looked scornfully at him and said, "Ben, Peter Donohoe is only an opportunist." Ben had forgotten the small matter of the Polo Grounds All-Ireland final in 1947 when the "opportunist" played a great part in Cavan's defeat of Kerry; his accuracy from frees earned him the nickname "The Babe Ruth of Gaelic Football" from an American writer.

It was only in this matter of Kerry football that Séamus de Faoite was deadly serious and partisan. He was one of the wits of Burgh Quay and kept the sub-editors' desk amused when he was in the mood. One night, Major Vivion de Valera, Managing Director and Editor in Chief of the group of newspapers, walked slowly through the old news-room (which was supposed to have been modelled on the *Daily Express* newsroom in Manchester) taking everything in. He paused at the door for one long, lingering look before leaving. Séamus, who seemed to be engrossed in his work, suddenly raised his head and said, "There goes my beloved son whom I have well placed."

The general tone and style of writing on gaelic games I found to be declamatory and bordering on the mock-heroic. As far as I can make out, the general guidelines were established by two men at the beginning of the century.

Father J.B. Dollard, who may also have helped to coin my pet aversion "the Gael", wrote the following lines in 1907:

Ye noble Gaels of Ireland
Fair Banba needs you all!
Stand by your suffering Sireland
And await the Battle-Call!
Then may your peaceful weapons
Be changed to shimmering steel,
And from your bristling vanguard
Dismayed oppression reel!

The other writer, P.J. Devlin (who also used the pen name "Celt") wrote the following piece on the youth of his friend Michael Cusack:

When no one was around he would make a nearby declivity his antagonist and hurl the ball up its steep side to meet it bounding down from ridge and rock with the delirious delight of a full-blooded, limb-strong young Gael.

It is interesting to read Joyce's famous introduction of the Citizen in Barney Kiernan's pub, with that piece of Devlin's in mind:

The figure seated on a large boulder at the foot of a round tower was that of a broadshouldered deepchested stronglimbed frankeyed redhaired . . . brawnyhanded hairylegged ruddyfaced sinewyarmed hero.

Over the years this curiously inflated and hyperbolical style read like a parody of the originals on which it was based rather than an imitation. Once upon a time I had several examples off by heart but was foolish enough not to commit them to paper while they were fresh in my memory. However, the following conveys the mood and style reasonably well:

The Short Grass man, a tower of strength in defence and a tiger in attack, stamped his mark indelibly on this game when, midway through the second moiety, he grabbed the leather, rounded the centre half-back, and sent a daisy-cutter past the baffled Breffny custodian.

A more recent example shows the pitfalls for the unwary which this kind of writing contains:

Such was the majesty of the Valentia islander that one could have been forgiven for thinking that he had eschewed the official ball and had substituted one of his own.

The local newspapers, as Myles na Gopaleen and Patrick Kavanagh were aware, contained gems of various kinds which would be considered too unsophisticated for the Dublin dailies to carry. I once possessed a copy of an open letter to the GAA authorities in Wicklow, which was published by the *Wicklow People*, written and signed by the mothers, sisters, wives and girlfriends of the Baltinglass senior football team. They wanted the authorities to note their anxiety that their loved ones would be maimed or murdered in front of their eyes by the Rathnew team and its savage supporters.

Another memento, which was not published in a paper but circulated privately, is a well-printed mortuary card bearing the following inscription:

WITH DEEP SORROW THE GWEEDORE GALLANTS
announce the
Passing of the Dungloe Dodgers
on Sunday, September 10th, 1961
Interment in O'Donnell Park Cemetery
May their hopes Rest in Pieces forever
Honorary Coffin Bearers — the Gallant Gallaghers,
Jackie Coyle, Owenie McBride and Padraig McBride.

The card was posted to the members and officials of the Dungloe team which had been beaten by Gweedore in a famous victory, and was the subject of at least two sermons in the respective parish churches.

But my own favourite report comes from the *Clare Champion* of some years back. It dealt with an abandoned match between Crusheen and Clarecastle and the reporter was clearly a disciple of the explosive opening:

Did the referee abandon the game or did Clarecastle walk off the field? These are but two of the imponderables surrounding last Sunday's controversial Clare senior hurling championship quarter-final tie between Clarecastle and Crusheen at Cusack Park, Ennis, which still hangs in the balance following an incident in the 20th minute which finished up with the referee (Mick Spain, Offaly) being escorted off the field by gardaí, and both teams retiring to the dressing rooms.

After a long and confused description of the incident in the Crusheen square, the reporter sums up as follows:

Who was wrong and who was right is a matter that will have to wait over for answering until after the referee's report is considered. But of one thing I am certain, and that is, no marks at all for the section of supporters on the sideline who saw fit to throw stones at Ml. Slattery as he lay injured on the ground, and to that certain section on the embankment whose derisive shouts did anything but encourage the players to hurl. This kind of stuff the GAA can well do without.

The following week it was announced that Clarecastle were threatening to withdraw from the championship if the referee's report was not to their satisfaction. There was also a hint that, perhaps, the Crusheen people were not too happy with the previous week's report. The reporter, in the interests of what RTE calls "balance", shows the other side of the coin:

175

The position in Crusheen is one of anxious waiting also. I have yet to meet a Crusheen man who will accept a walk-over, so determined are they that the game be contested on the field and not in the confines of a super-plush hotel-room where soft carpets and high-toned language are the order of the day. This is the sort of thing which one has come to expect from Crusheen, for behind the tough exterior which, at times, can put the heart crossways in opponents, lies a definite fair-play streak, which only shines out in extenuating circumstances such as this.

It reminded me of a match I once saw in Ballinasloe, at which a fight broke out. It was not particularly vicious, more a "hold me back before I open the bastard" type of fight rather than a real clattering match. But one player refused to be restrained and seemed determined to inflict damage on a certain opponent. Then an official of his club ran on to the field and dragged the wild one to the sideline shouting, "Don't get yourself put off, you bloody eejit. Can't you do him in the friendly in Loughrea in a fortnight?"

The reporting of "incidents", as they were still called, was very restrained in the fifties. The tone was set by Michael O'Hehir's radio commentaries and his famous phrase, "For the life of me I don't know what the booing is about."

His commentary on the All-Ireland football semi-final in 1946, between Kerry and Antrim, drove me to the verge of apoplexy. I was sitting in our house in Inis Mór, wishing I were in Croke Park, for I had seen some of the Antrim players in action and considered them to be really gifted. It was a wet day and the booing started early on, and I was familiar enough with games to know exactly what crowd reactions were about, particularly when frees for a certain team followed the booing.

Like everyone else in the country whose only link with the games was the radio, I was a fan of O'Hehir's and the fact that his father, like my own, was a Clareman, almost made him a relation. But all that changed that day and I could never again work up the same enthusiasm for his folksy technique which seemed to be aimed at providing entertainment for hospital patients rather than giving a complete picture of what was happening.

This game, which was one of the disgraces of the forties, was commented on in a magazine called *Spotlight on Sport* which was published by O'Hehir annually and to which I subscribed. This extract put the tin hat on things as far as I was concerned:

> The crowd did not like much of the Kerry defence methods, the pulling down of the players and the like, but frankly, while I am very strongly opposed to such tactics I thought the booing was carried a little too far. I take my hat off to the Antrim side who, after a quick rise to fame, almost qualified for the final. Their future is indeed bright and success would be popular.

As we know, their future was not bright and therefore the presumed popularity did not arise. Michael O'Hehir's attitude was typical of a period when it was not considered good for people to be told unpalatable things and the phrase "it is for your own good" was used to counter curiosity and make you feel that your interests were being paternalistically cared for.

One journalist who enjoyed tweaking the noses of the pompous was Joe Sherwood who, when I arrived in Burgh Quay, was writing a daily sports column for the *Evening Press* under the title "In The Soup". In his days as Sports Editor of the *Irish Press* Joe was reputed to have been involved in a bout of fisticuffs in the front office of the paper with a senior GAA official who had come in to complain about a report. If it happened it would have been to Joe's taste for he delighted in challenging people to wrestle him, Cumberland style.

He got under the skin of the IRFU while writing "In

The Soup" and in a fit of foolish peevishness they banned him from the press-box in Lansdowne Road. This did not trouble Joe one bit, in fact it gave him added status and he retaliated by christening the back row of one of the most fashionable club sides in Dublin, The Murder Squad, at which there was indeed "murder".

He was a great believer in letting the public write his column and that was also good for circulation. When he wanted to start a controversy he would ask a member of the staff to write a provocative letter, under an assumed name, and he would add an even more provocative reply which was enough to prime the pump and the letters flowed until Joe decided that the matter was done to death.

But on occasions he had a march stolen on him. Once, after the Dublin senior team had been defeated unexpectedly, he started a letters campaign complaining that St Vincent's was monopolising the Dublin team and that new blood from elsewhere was needed. Naturally, St Vincent's supporters rallied to the cause and the column was bursting with angry letters, pro and con. Through Joe's safety net swam one letter which caused great hilarity. It was written in the office and stated that the root of Dublin's present problem was at full back and would the selectors ever go and have a look at the best young player in that position in the county, one K. O'Shea who played for Parnell's.

Joe Sherwood was an old-fashioned journalist who called a spade a bloody shovel on occasions but was not even remotely related to the present-day crusader who constantly parades his own honesty and incorruptibility on all possible occasions. Personally, when I see a headline along the lines of "Humpty McDumpty tells how he was not killed in the Munich crash and calls for honesty in high places", I think of "Fear Ciúin".

"Fear Ciúin", who was as *ciúin* as Galway Bay in a force nine gale, was the chief gaelic games columnist for the *Sunday Press*. He delivered his copy to the Sports Editor personally, usually with the words, "I am lambasting the enemies of Gaeldom in style this week, Tommy". The *Sunday Press* pioneered an exaggerated type of lay-out which caused Patrick Kavanagh to say that when he opened the sports pages he was set upon by a series of leaping footballers with enlarged genitals while Behan said that he put on his steel helmet to protect himself from the bullets which screamed off the pages that dealt with every ambush from Soloheadbeg to the bloodier battles of the Civil War.

"Fear Ciúin" had a wonderful style. He once wrote that "Joe Salmon, at a comparatively early age has etched himself a niche in the annals of Gaeldom but should curb a tendency to propel the leather skywards." He sang the praises of the hard life when he and his comrades in Clare stripped in ditches that were awash with rain and mocked these weaklings who wanted hot water and showers. He was a staunch defender of the Ban and the real bane of his life was Eamonn Mongey, the Mayo star of the fifties team, who wrote another column for the paper in which he attacked the Ban regularly and caused "Fear Ciúin" to go into hysterics when he conducted a poll among players after a Railway Cup semi-final, which showed that twenty-eight of the thirty wished the Ban to be abolished immediately. "What right or authority did they have?" "Fear Ciúin" wanted to know, which was again an example of how children were supposed to be seen, patted on the head but not heard.

All that began to change in the sixties and it was in 1965 that the first novel, that I know of, that deals with the role of the GAA club in an Irish town was published. It is *Michael Joe* by William Cotter Murray from west Clare and is set in a small town that bears a strong resemblance to Miltown Malbay but is called Corrigbeg. Michael Joe McCarthy is a shopkeeper and football is one of his principal interests until an injury puts an end to his career as a local sporting hero.

The novel gives a realistic and often crude picture of

life in a small Irish town in the 1930s and the descriptions of the football matches are particularly vivid. Corrigbeg are at daggers drawn with their near neighbours, the Quilty team from a few miles away. Michael Joe is often in the wars:

In one fight he was tripped from behind and when he was on the ground got a kick in the head. Corrigbeg was playing Quilty, a team made up mainly of fishermen from two or three families in the neighbouring village to Corrigbeg. If one member of the Quilty team was roughed, all of them wanted to fight. Michael Joe kicked a Quilty man accidentally, and then fourteen other men ganged up on him before his own team could save him. That was when he got the kick in the head.

As a result of these activities, Michael Joe became a hero to everyone in Corrigbeg and girls stood at the back of the goal when he played at full back. He gets dirtier and more vicious and it is during another match against Quilty that he gets badly injured.

The Quiltonians soon saw that Michael Joe had to be knocked out if they were to win. From the sidelines came shouts of "Gut him, gut McCarthy" when he had the ball. And they went after him physically when they saw they could not beat him to the ball. He was tripped, shoved, elbowed, and kneed in the back and groin. The more the opposition attacked him physically, the better he played. He never once felt any of the blows that landed, though, by half-time, his body was a mass of bruises, and his shins were bleeding from cuts where he had been kicked.

Before the Quilty players knock him down and dance jigs on his body, Michael Joe had a new experience. He began to enjoy his suffering:

He was determined to keep the peace. He would not lose his head; whatever physical punishment the Quiltonians dealt out to him, he'd take peaceably. The role of the suffering martyr was balm to his spirit. He rose to new heights of football in the second half. He could almost see the *Clare Champion* reporter writing that he was "in the thick of the fray at all moments" and "all over the field, until it looked like there were fifteen Michael Joe McCarthys instead of one stalwart full-back".

Michael Joe is carried away with a smashed collar bone but as he lies in bed at home he hears a commotion in the street. Corrigbeg have won:

Old men, children, middle-aged men who used to be footballers and now played only in their imaginations and their talk, went up to Canada Cross to surround the victorious footballers, slap them on the back, inquire about the great moments of glory and who made them in the winning of the victory. And the women came too, the women who hated the football because it maimed their men, sapped their energy, usurped the love of their men, but who later learned to take their own pleasure in the victories of their men, though it sometimes meant their own loss. All traffic was stopped around the crossroads. The lazy, summer afternoon in the small town exploded.

11

Gradually I became industrious. During my first year in the *Irish Press* I began to broadcast regularly, became involved in writing for films and edited the monthly magazine *Comhar*. Economic pressure more than any change in character was responsible for this surge of activity. It was Donncha O Laoire from An Chomhdháil who asked me to work with him on a weekly programme for schools, *Ar Fud na Tíre*. As well as learning how to interview young people, a skill that can only be acquired through practical experience, I covered gaelic games in schools and the minor All-Irelands for the programme.

It was interesting to meet so many young players of promise and try to spot the ones who were most likely to become good seniors and those who were destined to be remembered as "great minors". The players I remember best, for reasons of personality as much as playing ability, are Jimmy Duggan of Galway, Des Foley of Dublin and Tom Walsh of Kilkenny, a brilliant blonde-haired hurler who later lost an eye in an unfortunate accident in an All-Ireland final.

I also remember Father Brendan Kavanagh of St Jarlath's College, who trained five successful Hogan Cup-winning teams. He remains in mind as much for the high standards of sportsmanship he demanded of his charges as for his undoubted skill as a trainer. But the most exciting colleges game I saw during that period, when I attended a match almost every Sunday during the season, was a

Harty Cup final in Cusack Park in Ennis, between St Flannan's College and Ennis CBS. I got so involved during the last quarter that I forgot to switch on my machine to record the commentary; which is another reason why I remained a spectator rather than become a full-time reporter or commentator.

Gael Linn had now become a very vital, if diffuse, organisation. It careered off in all directions. It had a fish-processing factory in Carna, an estate in Teelin, a theatre in the Damer Hall on St Stephen's Green, a hotel near Naas, a furniture factory in Navan, as well as producing records, radio programmes and a weekly newsreel.

At an early stage in its life I was asked to write the commentary for the newsreel, which was shown in cinemas as "Amharc Eireann". It happened at a time when the unfortunate use of a term, in an item on a National League hurling final, had alerted everyone concerned to the care which had to be taken when dealing with the written word which had then to be spoken to a cinema audience; many of whom had only the barest knowledge of Irish.

The writer used the correct dictionary term for a free in hurling, but when the audience heard of a "saorphoc" for Tipperary and another "saorphoc" for their opponents and yet another "saorphoc" for Tipperary, their hoots of laughter drowned the rest of the commentary. In Burgh Quay, at the time, we were recovering from the impact of a heading which slipped past all defences and appeared on the Christmas cookery page: "How to stuff your bird for Christmas." Such was the invincible innocence of the perpetrator that nobody was prepared to instruct her in the broader use of language, but those in her vicinity were cautioned to exercise the dirtier side of their minds in future.

This skill of fitting words to pictures, and of using words to add a dimension to visual images, has as much to do with mechanics as linguistics. For me it is one of the pleasures of writing, but I notice that all the best practical manuals on the subject are produced in the United

States where writing is regarded as much a craft as a product of divine, or malign, inspiration. Colm O Laoghaire and Jim Mulkerns schooled me in this work, and I was taken many steps further during a long working-relationship with Louis Marcus.

Louis came from Cork to make films for Gael Linn and, among the first, were two instructional films on football and hurling, made with the assistance of Players-Wills: "Peil" and "Christy Ring". My own role as commentary writer enabled me to watch, from my sideline seat, all the old tensions between Gael Linn and the top brass of the GAA emerge again from the shadows. A series of niggling rows, bureaucratic forms of tripping and jersey-pulling, delayed the production of both films.

Letters from Gael Linn went astray on their way to Croke Park and were too late to be discussed at a particular meeting; or they were addressed to the wrong council or board; or were considered so important that a special meeting had to be convened to discuss their implications fully. Like many such forms of unarmed civil war in Ireland this row seemed to be about the making of the films but was really about other unspoken matters.

At the time, I saw Gael Linn's position much more clearly than I could see, or indeed find out, what the GAA was up to. With the benefit of hindsight I can now see a fuller picture.

Gael Linn, not being an organisation with branches in all parts of the country, believed in getting the right man in the right place and getting him to work his miracle at the right moment. Seán O Síocháin, who was Paddy O'Keefe's assistant at the time, was the Gael Linn trustee with responsibility for handling the GAA. Máirtín O Cadhain, until he resigned amid sparks of acrimony, was the trustee with responsibility for the Gaeltacht and allied matters.

The GAA, keenly aware of its position as the senior national organisation that never split, and a highly graduated organisation at that, resented this Johnny-come-lately that was trying to wheel the GAA to its own advantage by taking possession of one of the chief spokes. The answer was to slow everything down to a standstill and to be seen to be in control of the situation and calling the shots. And of course there was the inevitable clash of personalities between Paddy O'Keefe and Dónal Ó Móráin. Even when the films were eventually made, Seán O Síocháin was forced to resign as a trustee of Gael Linn and a most exalted GAA personage was unable to continue as a trustee of Mater Hospital pools, which were run on cross-channel soccer, when it became clear that he would get a belt of the Ban in the ribs from Gael Linn if he did.

It was all good dirty fun. But it struck me at the time, as it did many times before and since, that certain organisations would prefer their objectives to perish in failure rather than see them achieved by an organisation other than themselves and by methods of which they did not approve.

But soon after the GAA allowed the film to slip its moorings it ran aground on a sandbank of Kerry duplicity. It had been decided to make the Kerry football team, then in training for the 1960 All-Ireland final, the centre-piece of the film. At first this seemed to be going according to plan and the crew began work in Killarney with the blessing of everyone from the Central Council to the Kerry County Board.

Then some of the players decided to engage in spoiling tactics of their own. They were prepared to co-operate, but they were not co-operating, but there was absolutely no row with the film-makers. It was very reminiscent of the murder trial that earned me red ears in the pub in Waterville. A lot of the evidence centred on a shot which was, or was not, heard at a particular time which varied because both daylight saving time and winter time were used simultaneously in the area; and used to even greater effect during the trial. Towards the end of the long hearing, as yet another witness arrived on the stand, a weary prosecuting counsel decided to take a short-cut and come directly to the point:

"Now, about this shot . . ." he began.

"What shot?" demanded the witness.

It took some days before the target for the Killarney shot emerged clearly. Some of the players wanted Dr Eamonn O'Sullivan, long-time trainer of the team but now in dispute with the County Board, to appear in the training sequences. Work was held up for days as the players tried to use the film as a stick with which to beat the County Board into reinstating Dr O'Sullivan as team trainer. The crew had to depart, much wiser in the ways of the Kingdom.

Of course the Kerry team did appear in the climax of "Peil", which shows Down's historic victory over them in the 1960 final. But people still remark on Mick O'Connell's absence from the instructional sequences in which Seán Purcell and Frank Stockwell of Galway, Seán O'Neill and Leo Murphy of Down, Greg Hughes of Offaly, Kevin Behan of Louth and Kevin Heffernan of Dublin demonstrate different basic skills. O'Connell was not alone the outstanding mid-fielder of his day, he was regarded as one of the most graceful and gifted ball players of all time. Short of promising to tow Croke Park south and moor it at Portmagee, every possible inducement was offered to persuade him to appear. It was the film's loss at the time and the long-term loss to an understanding of his great talents does not need to be emphasised. But all that took place during his shy islander period which later changed as he entered public life with some success.

The other participants were as co-operative as GAA players and officials at that particular level always are, in my experience. That nothing more advanced than "Peil" has been made in the intervening quarter century, tells its own tale of the GAA's practical regard for the traditions they guard so fiercely with their official mouths.

The making of "Christy Ring" was also held up for a period by the same official red tape and the efforts of a few troglodytes in the Cork County Board to make even more trouble. But once work began it proceeded rapidly and happily to its conclusion.

Louis Marcus published a series of articles in the *Irish Times*, in October 1964, describing how the film was made and how he came to know and admire the man for his dedication to his craft and his ability to break his skills down into their basic elements. If the film proved anything, apart from capturing Christy Ring in action for all time, it was that the GAA should have moved mountains in an effort to appoint him national hurling coach. Not alone was he a wonderful practitioner of this great game but he was also a born teacher, with endless patience and a most sardonic sense of humour which found expression in short, laconic statements.

When I was introduced to him by Louis Marcus and Pádraig Tyers when the time had come to write the commentary for the instructional section of the film, I was as nervous as I was when making my first live broadcast. He came to the point quickly: how was the job going to be done? I told him that he would have to explain all his actions in the various sequences, emphasise what was important at each stage, and that I would find the exact words to convey this to the audience.

He thought about it for a little time and then, sliding down off the table on which he had been sitting, in the Gael Linn office in the Grand Parade, began to talk at a great rate, walking around the room, changing direction frequently when emphasising a point by swivelling on the balls of his very small and shapely feet which contrasted with the large hands and thick wrists and forearms. He knew exactly what he wanted to stress and having discussed the filming in detail with Louis knew where the slow motion and stop-action sequences occurred.

In fact, when he found out that slow motion filming used twice the amount of film that usually goes through the camera, he said that this was terrible waste and then said, with a little smile, "If you had told me that when we were doing it I would have slowed everything down myself."

187

We then went off to the Mardyke where he went through the taking of a sideline cut, showing me what he had explained in the office and asking a lot of questions. He did not tog out but hit every ball as if he were playing in a match. Obviously, he wanted the film to be as perfect as possible and did not care how much trouble he was put to in order to ensure its success.

Afterwards, when we had worked out a scheme for the scripting, we went to the Oyster for a meal and then I walked along Patrick Street with him towards the Fountain Cafe where he lived at the time. It was during this short walk that I saw another side of his nature.

During a match against UCC the previous Sunday, the player who had been marking Christy had his wrist broken. It happened as a result of a fall but that did not stop the spread of rumours. Along the other side of the street came a gaggle of students, eating chips and talking loudly. When they spotted Christy they began to taunt him with shouts of "Dirty Ring".

To my surprise, Christy rushed into the street, head stuck out like an angry gander, and let fly a string of abuse causing the students to run to a safer point, near the Savoy Cinema, from which they continued their hooting. I was embarrassed by the incident, but even more surprised that he should pay any attention to them.

"Did you hear that?" he demanded.

I said that they were young fellows with a few drinks aboard, looking for cheap amusement, and that he should ignore them. I did not say that I could easily imagine them telling an exaggerated version of the incident, gleefully, in the digs later on.

"That's all you know, then," said Christy in a fury. "You probably think that I'm a respected man in this town. There are people in this town, boy, that think I'm locked up in the red house on the hill all week and only let out to hurl on Sundays."

This sudden blast of realism nearly sent me staggering through the nearest shop window, for during my years on the road I too had heard the various tall tales which made up part of the folklore of Christy Ring. Some of it reminded me of the stories I heard in Sligo about the magical traditional fiddler, Michael Coleman. What did surprise me was that Christy was aware of it himself. But the subject changed rapidly when a journalist from the *Cork Examiner* came towards us and hailed Christy.

"Keep your mouth shut you and keep walking," hissed Ring to me. "This fellow's only looking for a story and he's not going to get it." It must be said that he did not have a lot of respect for journalists and their much-vaunted integrity, so I changed the subject without telling about my mother and Comrade Lenin.

The work progressed very smoothly and Christy went over the script with me, again and again, until we were both completely satisfied that the instructions and explanations were as accurate, clear and concise as we could make them. After that it was vetted by Louis Marcus and spoken by Pádraig Tyers. It is a piece of work that affords me great satisfaction every time I hear it, although the sound of Christy's voice introducing each particular skill in his laconic fashion saddens me.

For it was a particularly happy job and everyone involved has his own memories of Christy and his remarks. His humour could be very pointed, particularly where hurling was concerned. He did a very realistic imitation of a contemporary who had a habit of holding his head very low as he ran for a ground ball. Ring claimed he was almost blind and could only locate the ball by the sound it made as it came near him.

He also told a story of a team-mate who once hit Mick Mackey a blow of his fist; as much out of cowardice as aggression, according to Ring. To the player's horror, Mackey only staggered slightly and then took off in pursuit of his assailant threatening to maim him.

"I declare to God," said Christy, "he went around the pitch twice before a crowd of players stopped Mackey and the only thing that was stopping our fella from running home to Cork was the paling around the ground."

His dedication to the game of hurling was total and took in the whole country. He admired Joe Salmon greatly for keeping hurling alive in Connacht during the lean years. But he could also be scathing. One back on whom he played regularly he described to me as "a complete pig". When asked about another back's ability as a hurler he replied, "He's not a hurler, he's a calamity."

His toughest battles were against Tipperary, and the dispute over the reporting of the incident with Tom Moloughney, in the Munster Final of 1961, caused even more of a rumpus in the press than the Mickey Burke incident in 1953. This time Ring was at war with the journalists who had accused him of hitting Moloughney, who retired injured.

Most of the journalists present in Limerick were satisfied that they saw Ring, who had previously been involved in hostilities with John Doyle, hit Moloughney. A full account of the matter is given by Val Dorgan in his book. I was not in Limerick but I remember Mick Dunne's report from Limerick being discussed in the *Irish Press* office that Sunday night. Mick Dunne named Ring but Pádraig Puirséal, who was on the sub-editor's desk, advised the editor that hurlers had strange second throughts on occasions and that it would be safer, from a legal viewpoint, not to name Christy Ring; it was clear, though, from the report that he was the offending player and in those days readers were used to drawing their own conclusions from a series of heavy hints in sports reports.

Seán Og O Ceallacháin based his Sunday night radio report on the day's results on a carbon copy of Mick Dunne's unedited report, and named Ring; as did John D. Hickey in his report for the *Irish Independent*. Both RTE and the *Irish Independent* subsequently retracted and apologised to Christy Ring. To make a long story short, Ring denied having struck Moloughney, Moloughney could not identify the player who struck him and there were dark rumours that an un-named Cork player was willing to swear that he and not Ring hit Moloughney, if the case went to court. It all goes to show that Pádraig Puirséal was a wise old owl. And it also goes to show that the GAA had not learned any lessons since the affair of 1953, for they declared war on the journalists, particularly John D. Hickey, and did nothing to get to the bottom of the affray in Limerick.

These events occurred over a year before the making of the film and put one remark of Ring's in an interesting light. He was talking about the different styles of hurling played in different counties and was asked to name the best, Cork excepted. He thought for a while and then said, "You can say what you like but the only team you can hurl all out against is Tipperary." He meant it as a compliment.

But while I found his dedication to hurling admirable, his skills formidable and his company most congenial, I must confess that I found his fierce competitiveness repellent and somewhat frightening. It did not apply to hurling only. Winning in any sport he took up, was of the utmost importance to him. This attitude is beyond my own comprehension and seems to enter the realm of fanaticism.

Only on one occasion do I remember him talking about football, which he played at club level with St Nicholas's. He regarded it, as indeed did Michael Cusack, as an inferior game to hurling. He said he had little time for players whom he saw described by sports writers (still harping on them) as artists and stylists. Unless they were able to lift their team when the team needed their skills most, but were only good when, as he put it, "cycling down the hill with the wind in their backs," they had no business playing a competitive team game. He mentioned two players whom he thought to have this essential quality: Seán Purcell of Galway and Paddy Doherty of Down.

Seán Purcell would have to be included in any short-list of great footballers, if only for having played with such brilliance in so many different positions. A natural forward, or mid-fielder, since his days as a colleges star, and a deadly free-taker, he probably played his best game for Galway at full-back and against a great Mayo team.

His understanding with his fellow Tuam-man, Frank Stockwell, was recorded on film in the 1956 All-Ireland final, when Stockwell established the record for the highest individual score from play in a 60-minute All-Ireland. Completely different in physique, style of play and even temperament, their unique and totally unselfish combination will always be remembered in GAA lore as the tale of "The Terrible Twins". Their particular attraction for writers and followers was strengthened by the fact that their sportsmanship was as outstanding as their flamboyant skills.

Paddy Doherty was an essential part of the Down plan to win an All-Ireland by 1961, for which due credit must be given to the county secretary, Maurice Hayes, who put the plan into action and hit the target a year ahead of schedule.

So far in my lifetime, Down have been the most exciting team to come out of the vast wilderness of gaelic football, at county level, and to make it to the very top. Doherty, who was working at his trade in London, must have lost a lot of overtime flying home at weekends to play in challenge matches all over the country as part of the plan to gain experience. I first saw Down play Dublin in an evening match in Croke Park about 1958, and although they were beaten you could tell that they were a coming team. They were strong, very fast, good in the air, and full of the self-assurance that annoyed some of the traditionalists. They also produced one of the greatest forwards of all time: the elegant Seán O'Neill.

"Fear Ciúin" lambasted the Down team in the *Sunday Press* for wearing black togs, which seemed to remind him of soccer, and for organising an annual dinner dance instead of the traditional céilí; which everyone knew was only called a céilí to escape the GAA ruling on foreign dances. But one has to take more seriously the lambasting of a contemporary, Mick O'Dwyer, who had the following to say in the *Kerry GAA Yearbook* in 1976:

I think Down did a lot of damage to Gaelic football. They broke the ball a lot and they played it very close and marked tightly. They weren't playing the ball that much but they played the man quite a lot. I suppose it paid dividends for them. They fouled men in the centre of the field — and won All-Irelands with it. But it was not a good thing for the game.

When I showed this to a Kerry friend, an expert in matters pertaining to gaelic football, he assured me — without twinkle, tremor or smile — that Down invented off-the-ball fouling as far as gaelic football was concerned. This sent me post-haste to a telephone. My Down friend remained a lot cooler than I had imagined. He attributed the criticism to the fact that Down had the audacity to come to Croke Park from nowhere and beat the Kingdom at their first attempt, without seeing fit to ask the Kingdom authorities to stamp their passports, and repeated the process twice again in the same decade.

"If you use that squirt of sour grape juice in your book," he said, "do please introduce it as coming from the Kingdom that kicked Antrim off the park in 1946, put Tommy Murphy in hospital and roughed Larry Stanley out of football."

Armagh, in 1953, was the other team from the Six Counties that came closest to winning an All-Ireland final but, like Derry in 1958, they lacked the scoring forwards without whom All-Irelands will not be won. The Tyrone team of 1956 and 1957 did have scoring forwards and would probably have won an All-Ireland had they not met Galway at their best in 1956 and Louth at their best the following year. Tyrone were a very fast team, right out from the back line, and had a match-winner in Iggy Jones.

I have written earlier that the rules of gaelic football were useless when it came to protecting such a fast, slight player. In the *Donegal GAA Yearbook* for 1982 an old county player, now deceased, explained, with an honesty uncharacteristic of players when these matters are discussed, how he and the Donegal full-back decided to take Iggy Jones out of a game by "sandwiching" him. "He was carried off. You had to do it, he was that good." A left-handed compliment to Iggy Jones but, as my Clare scribe put it, "no marks at all" to the GAA for permitting such conduct to go unpunished and for not putting their rules and their system of refereeing in order.

One remembers teams, units and individuals. For instance, the Meath team that won the All-Irelands of 1949 and 1954 had the best full-back line I have seen: Micheál O'Brien, Paddy O'Brien and Kevin McConnell, who also played together for Leinster before the Railway Cup competition became an anachronism. But whether Paddy O'Brien was a better full-back than Mayo's great Paddy Prendergast, Louth's Eddie Boyle, or Kerry's Joe Keohane or Joe Barrett, will always be a matter for endless and futile discussion. We spent hours picking teams in school and arguing about players we had never seen. It passed the time.

My own clear memory of football begins with the great Mayo, Meath, Kerry and Cavan teams of the early fifties and all the various county stars who lived in Dublin and played with Seán McDermott's, Clann na nGael, Peadar Macken's, Geraldines, Garda, Westerns and Erin's Hope, and wonderfully rugged matches between them and the rising St Vincent's and the long-established O'Toole's: contests which represented the constant strife between "Town and Culchie". Someone should write the history of club football in Dublin, covering the years up to the time when changing social and economic conditions made it possible for country players, resident in Dublin, to play with their own parish clubs and Dublin club football (and what exists in hurling) became truly representative of the city.

Mention of Cavan and Mayo brings me clearly up against the decline of gaelic football, which I will deal with briefly later. For if the Meath full-back line was the best I have seen was there ever a better half-back line than that of P.J. Duke, John Joe O'Reilly and Simon Deignan? Could Mick Higgins, Tony Tighe and Peter

Donohoe of Cavan, and Pádraig Carney, Mick Flanagan and Tom Langan of Mayo, be left out of the reckoning when the best forwards of the last thirty-five years are named? Still, Mayo won their last All-Ireland in 1951 and Cavan their last in 1952.

Apart from Down the only other team to come in from exterior darkness has been Offaly. Like their hurlers, who followed them some years later, I find their outstanding characteristic to be an unwillingness to countenance defeat, particularly when they reach the final stage of any competition. Willie Bryan was a player of class and Martin Furlong must rank with Charlie Nelligan of Kerry, Paddy Cullen of Dublin, Johnny Geraghty of Galway and Ollie Crinnigan of Kildare as the most consistent goalkeepers I have seen.

But for both brilliance and consistency one would have to put the Kerry team of the seventies and eighties, the Dublin team of the same period and the Galway team of the sixties, in a class apart. And having said it one must also say that the Sam Maguire has not gone to Connacht since Galway won the last of their three-in-a-row, in 1966, nor to Ulster since Down won in 1968; and that twelve of the All-Irelands played since 1968 have been won by Kerry and Dublin between them. (The others were won by Offaly, three times, and Cork once.)

It can be fairly said that Kerry and Dublin have been the life-support machine of gaelic football for a decade, earning the big money for the GAA and showing what gaelic football at its best can be, as a game and a spectacle. The Kerry forwards, over that period, are the best attacking unit I have seen, and Mike Sheehy their king. Although one hesitates before coming to a definite conclusion about a player who still has years ahead of him, an exception has to be made in the case of Jack O'Shea. He is a great one.

Earlier, I spoke of the Galway hurler, Billy Duffy, as a potentially great centre half back. Dublin's Kevin Moran showed every sign of becoming one of the great centre halves of all time before he joined Manchester United. He may never be rated as highly as a soccer player as he would have been in gaelic football had he not gone abroad, but he took with him one characteristic which is in short supply in international soccer at present. There are various words used to describe it but a well-known English sports-writer put it like this: "Kevin Moran never hesitates to put his head where most players would hesitate to put their boot."

The major share of the credit for what has happened to Dublin football, at county level, since 1974, must go to Kevin Heffernan who persuaded Jimmy Keaveney to come out of retirement and become the keel of a new ship which was built in record time. Another "opportunist" like Big Peter Donohoe, Keaveney could almost put the ball through the eye of a needle, from a free or from play.

Heffernan was a very cerebral player and is generally regarded as the best left corner forward of modern times. He is as busy as an executive in a Semi-State body as Mick O'Dwyer is in private enterprise, but both of them have devoted almost all of their free time to the practical pro-motion of the game they served so well as players.

I also remember Kevin Heffernan as a very effective hurler with St Vincent's, at a time when a county final would draw a crowd of 25,000 or more. Faughs, New Ireland and Young Ireland were peppered with great players from all the hurling counties of Ireland and it was said that they had representatives at Kingsbridge Station offer-ing jobs in Dublin firms to young hurlers arriving in the city for the first time as "signing-up" fees!

The decline of hurling in Dublin saddens me much more than the decline of football nationally; not only because I regard hurling as more important but also because I see it as the neglected game. Perhaps if Dublin had won the 1961 All-Ireland hurling final against Tipperary, hurling would have continued to flourish in the city. It was a native-born Dublin team, powered by Des Foley at mid-field, and they could have won had they not allowed the antics of a loutish Tipperary player to distract them.

It has now declined to the point when nothing short of a high-powered campaign, over a period of ten years, will restore it to its old strength. As it is constituted at present, I cannot see the GAA facing up to this problem with the necessary speed. It might be a good idea, as Mícheál O Muircheartaigh has suggested, to persuade Kevin Heffernan to leave the footballers in Tony Hanahoe's hands for a period and get him to plan and to launch the hurling revival. All it takes is imagination, but when did you last see a flash of that commodity from the direction of Croke Park?

12

The Wexford hurling team, those gigantic men who burst into the fifties to invest the game with a new magic, gave me more pleasure than any other team I have seen in any code. They had a quality which cannot be accurately defined, even by those involved in show-business who use the term most: "star quality".

It owed something to their very size, although some of them were not very tall; it had something to do with the three Rackard brothers from Killane; it had a lot to do with their deserved reputation for sportsmanship and it owed something to their intensely loyal and good-humoured followers who supported them, good days and bad, in huge numbers. It was my own good fortune, through dexterous manipulation of my mobility, to see most of their matches in the early fifties when they were seeking the county's first All-Ireland since 1910.

They have won many famous victories since 1951, when they won the Leinster Championship and the Oireachtas Tournament final, including four All-Irelands, but I remember Wexford best for winning the most extraordinary hurling match I have ever seen: the 1956 National League final against Tipperary, in Croke Park.

It was played in a gale which favoured Tipperary in the first half. Wexford played badly and lost their captain, Jim English, with a head-injury. But for the superhuman efforts of Bobby Rackard, Tipperary would have been over the hill and far away at half time. As it was they led by 2-10 to Wexford's lone point. I thought it was all over but the Wexford supporters on the Cusack Stand assured me that if Nicky Rackard could get going early in the second half the match could still be won. I admired their faith but doubted their judgement.

Then the second half started and it was unbelievable. Nicky Rackard belted in two goals and a point and the two great mid-fielders, the blonde Ned Wheeler and the dark Jim Morrissey, began to pick off points from inside their own half of the field.

The half was played in an atmosphere of mounting hysteria as Tipperary fought hard to retain the lead. Paddy Kenny scored four points against the gale, but there was little they could do against a side that could put over points from 80 yards; in fact Jim Morrisey scored one point from just outside his own 21-yard line!

Wexford got their nose ahead and won by 5-9 to 2-14 but for me the real star of the hour was Bobby Rackard who held the team together when it threatened to dis-integrate during the Tipperary bombardment in the first half.

One day in Nowlan Park, Wexford were trying hard to topple Kilkenny from their perch and for a long time looked like succeeding. Suddenly, there was a flurry of goals and the tide turned. The Kilkenny supporters, who had been almost silent for so long, now began to bay for Wexford's blood: "Stitch it into the Yellow-Bellies," they roared. The term was not new to me. I knew its origin was linked to a team of Wexford hurlers who went to play against a Cornish side centuries before, and who tied yellow sashes around their waists to distinguish friend from foe.

But the bitter reply of the Wexford supporters in my vicinity, now sensing that defeat was going to be their lot, took me completely by surprise. "Who pissed in the pow-der?" they shouted at the Kilkenny supporters, who were moved to use very strong language indeed, and a few blows were exchanged here and there before the match ended.

One night in the *Irish Press* Pádraig Puirséal explained it all to me.

It was believed in Wexford that when the rebellion of 1798 collapsed, some of the insurgents tried to make their way to the safety of the Wicklow mountains. Marching by night, they arrived in Castlecomer at dawn and went down a mine to sleep through the day. While they slept, the Wexford version of the story goes, the miners urinated in their supply of powder and then sent for the Yeomen, who captured the Wexfordmen without difficulty as their muskets would not fire.

But in Ireland of the tribal spites very few things are that simple. When I wrote the story in my column in the *Sunday Press* an irate retired schoolmaster, from the Castlecomer area, wrote to correct me. According to him, the offending miners were not from Castlecomer at all but were Welshmen (would you believe it?) who had come to teach mining techniques to the locals. It was not his first time, he said, trying to catch up with this particular lie and pin it down for good.

I did my little bit but felt that it was futile and rather like doing what the miners — either Welsh or Kilkenny — had done, into a force nine gale of folk-memory. After all, it happened a mere 150 years previously and only about three or four hundred years after the Wexfordmen went to play in Cornwall and today's Wexford jersey contains a band of yellow.

Everywhere I went the GAA was giving me insights into history and folklore, making the past a very vital part of the present on a hot Sunday afternoon in Nowlan Park and many other parks and fields. Yet, there was no history of the GAA readily available and hardly anything at all about the GAA in the standard history books. Indeed Edmund Curtis, in his very fine history of Ireland, did not see fit to mention the GAA at all.

The GAA seemed very happy to leave its founder, Michael Cusack, in exterior darkness. They named a stand and two pitches after him, erected a monument over the family grave in Glasnevin and left it to those who wrote their dreary pageants to resurrect him as a Cúchulainn-like symbol and then shove him quickly back into his tomb.

Unlike the young man in Corkery's *Hidden Ireland*, who when called a fool publicly answered back angrily, "I am no fool, I know my genealogy," the GAA seemed willing to live with an incomplete pedigree and a cosy, if misconceived image of itself.

My active interest in these matters was brought to the boil by the series of Thomas Davis Lectures, "The Shaping of Modern Ireland", edited by Conor Cruise O'Brien, broadcast by Radio Eireann in 1955-56, and published in 1960. I well remember listening to Dr O'Brien's introductory lecture, on the period 1891 — 1916, and how the following passage excited me:

Some of the movements which were now emerging into importance had their beginnings in the Parnell period itself. One of these, and not the least notable, was the GAA, some of whose members, armed with their hurley sticks, formed Parnell's bodyguard in the last tumultuous meetings. In the 90's and early 1900's the GAA built on the ground cleared by the Land League: that is to say that it organised with faith and enthusiasm the replacement, among the young in many parts of the country, of what had been a servile spirit by a spirit of manliness and freedom. It was a new monument and one not erected by a grateful tenantry. More than the Gaelic League, more than Arthur Griffith's Sinn Féin, more than even the Transport and General Workers' Union and of course more than the movement which created the Abbey Theatre; more than any of these the Gaelic Athletic movement aroused the interest of large numbers of ordinary people throughout Ireland. One of the most successful and original mass-movements of its day, its importance has perhaps not even yet been fully recognised. Not that it has not received its full share of conventional praise; that, many friends ensure. But the tribute which it has not received is the more serious one of sustained critical attention; in this context it is perhaps necessary to say that what I mean by "critical" is not hostile but intelligent and, as far as possible, disinterested and dispassionate.

That is a fine statement and stands the test of time; although the suggested work still remains to be done. It must be noted, however, that when the above passage was read to the author, in the course of a radio programme broadcast during the GAA Centenary Congress in Belfast, his only comment was to say that the GAA contained more Provos than any other organisation in the country. When reminded that it also contained more Gardaí than any organisation other than An Garda Síochána, he chose to ignore the implications of the comment and instead exercised his current obsession around Casement Park. "Disinterested and dispassionate" indeed; rather a portrait of the historian as a propagandist.

It goes to show that even when the Good Fairy comes to the christening to wish the lucky child to be the brightest boy in school, there is always the possibility that the Bad Fairy will foul the font to ensure that the child also carries within him the worst characteristics of the school toady.

In his own contribution, "Michael Cusack and the Rise of the GAA", David Greene tried to give some substance to the shadowy figure of the founder. He also dealt concisely and well with the key issue of Fenian involvement in the early years of the Association, which in turn led to a question which exercises the attention of members of the GAA up to the present day. It is usually called "The GAA and Politics" but that is a kind of Gaelic euphemism for "The GAA and the continuing struggle for the unity of the Irish people, in peace, equality and harmony, and particularly between the Nationalists who advocate different methods for arriving at roughly the same solution." It is cumbersome, but a lot more accurate than the shorthand version.

This is a personal memoir and not a history, but as I happen to have some material relevant to these matters, and not generally available, I propose to include it in this chapter. It comes from the *Celtic Times*, the weekly paper published by Cusack for a year after his dismissal as secretary of the organisation he founded, in July 1886. It has been generally assumed by historians, including David Greene and Cusack's biographer, an Bráthair Liam O Caithnia, that all copies of Cusack's paper vanished without trace. It was my good fortune, some time ago, to gain access to an almost complete file of the *Celtic Times*. It is in private ownership, may be the only one in existence, and the owner, who wishes to remain anonymous, was kind enough to allow me to read through it and make notes. I very much hope that it will eventually find a permanent home in the National Library. There is little enough material to illuminate this area of this particular period in our history.

As I was one of the people who urged Liam O Caithnia to write his book on Cusack, I should state that my only disagreement with the work is his declaration of war on Joyce's Citizen and his efforts to prove that Cusack was not a heavy drinker. The Citizen in *Ulysses* is a fictional character based loosely on Cusack, who obviously made a great impression on Joyce. He appears in *Stephen Hero, Portrait of the Artist as a Young Man* and is mentioned twice in *Finnegans Wake.* If the GAA had paid half that much attention to him we would know a lot more about him today.

Readers who share my passion for trifles to decorate my magpie's nest will be interested to know that Croke Park is also mentioned in the *Wake* (*all the kules in kroukaparka*: na cúil i bPáirc an Chrócaigh) and I think the following, from the same book, would make a fine enigmatic banner for members of the Fingallians club to take on to Hill 16: *and Dub did glow that night. In Fingal of victories.*

It was unwise of Liam O Caithnia to get involved in

what I would classify as opposition to the "Portrait of the Patriot as a Poove or a Piss-Artist" school of popular Irish history. Being a rather wayward Paddy myself, I do not much care if the great men and women in Irish history had feet of clay extending to their very arm-pits, so long as the brain-boxes were working.

Without Cusack, the GAA would not have happened. His industry was amazing. The year after the GAA was founded he was teaching and managing his grinding school and was married with a young family of six. He wrote at least one article a week for *The Shamrock*. He was treasurer of Aontacht na Gaeilge and *Irisleabhar na Gaeilge*, secretary of the GAA, and wrote a weekly column on GAA affairs for *United Ireland*. It was this impossible work-load, coupled with his habit of firing off letters while in a rage, that led to his democratic dismissal from his position in the GAA after an earlier reprimand seemed to have offended him so much that he failed to carry out his secretarial duties responsibly. He left without seriously attempting to defend himself and in January 1887 he started the *Celtic Times*; not to attack the organisation that had fired him but, in an extraordinarily un-Irish way, to defend it from its internal and external enemies and preserve its unity at all costs.

In this Centenary Year I have read that the Davin family feel that Maurice Davin and his role in the founding of the GAA has been largely ignored by the GAA. Others have implied that Cusack's nationalism is more acceptable to those who control the GAA than Davin's. This in turn implies that Cusack was closer to the Fenians, if indeed he was not a Fenian, and that Davin was a good constitutionalist. It is clear from the *Celtic Times* that Cusack's only criticism of Davin concerned his reluctance to stand up to those who almost succeeded in wrecking the GAA in 1887.

I feel that a lot of what is written about this matter is an effort by politically motivated people to find reflections of their present attitudes in the past.

In the issue of 21 May, 1887, an article headed "Mr Maurice Davin's Resignation", signed by Michael Cusack, appeared in the *Celtic Times*. It dealt with the meeting in Hayes' Hotel, in Thurles, at which the GAA was founded:

For all practical purposes there were only two men at the meeting, and their names stand at the head of this article in the order in which I succeeded in placing them that day. There were in my opinion only two men in Ireland fit to occupy the President's Chair and only one man capable of acting as secretary. Mr Davin's broad view on every national question, kindly disposition and generous nature, as well as his widespread popularity among athletes, of every class and creed, not only in the British Isles but in America and Australia, justified me in pressing him to accept the responsibility of the Presidency. On the other hand, I believed that no man should fight the enemies of National pastimes but a secretary, and I knew no man able or willing to do this but myself. I fully realised the strength and intensity of the allied forces against which it would be the duty of the Chief Secretary to contend, if he desired to succeed: and I knew no man except myself, who had sufficient courage to fight the battle out to its bitterest end, for the bitterness of those I knew is said to be the quintessence of sweetness compared with mine, when I attack those who persistently assail a National movement with which I am identified. I was elected Secretary. Circumstances with which the public are fairly acquainted, led to my ceasing to discharge the duties of my office in March, 1886, but not before the Association had swept all opposition aside. With the President I did a little work in the first weeks of Summer, but it was only with the two objects of wiping out every trace of opposition to the GAA and of revising the rules before giving younger heads the opportunity of displaying their organising, controlling and fighting powers.

At the request of six members of the executive –

three of whom have since resigned — *United Ireland* struck Gaelic news out of its columns and a little later I was called on to resign, if I may believe the report that appeared in the public press. I carefully watched the proceedings of those who evidently wished to grab the Association. I cared not who managed it, so long as Mr Davin was at its head, for his presence there would be sufficient guarantee that the services of those who cater for avowed anti-nationalists would not be required. I had no desire whatever to appear before the public, nor would I intrude now, were I not convinced that Mr Davin's resignation threatens to rend the Association into fragments. Early this year, I warned P.N. Fitzgerald (*a prominent IRB figure who was to play a prominent part in the split at the Thurles Convention later that year*) that there were two parties in the GAA. What a Member of Parliament might call an astute but unscrupulous intelligence was steering it into the office of a newspaper which is notoriously identified with betting (*a weekly subsidiary of "The Freeman's Journal" called "Sport"*); and an honester but less capable party was rushing it ahead faster and further than I deemed advisable at the time (*the IRB faction*). The unscrupulous party have coolly, and in the broad light of day, taken the road I saw them shodding their hooves for; and the other party has shown more incapacity and an infinitely more impoverished and evanescent National spirit than I gave them credit for possessing.

I will not hear that Mr Davin will retire while this most undesirable condition of things lasts. He labours under one great disadvantage. He lives far from the centres of intrigues. Those are brought to a focus in Dublin. He was the first man to reply over his name to an article which I wrote in *United Ireland* in October 1884 (*calling for an organisation for native games to be set up*). I want to be even with him.

I am at present supported by a well-knit band of Gaelic volunteers, who can sweep the country every week. What they collect I can boil down for Maurice Davin. The information I can supply will enable him to outflank all the enemy's movements. I would suggest that an extraordinary general meeting of representatives of affiliated clubs be called at once to consider Mr Davin's resignation, and that no business be transacted at the meeting but that of which the delegates shall have got at least two week's notice.

The piece speaks for itself and it shows, among other things, that to say that the GAA got involved in politics — at any particular stage of its development up to, and including, the present day — is putting the cart before the horse. Politics were there from the beginning, deeply involved in the GAA. David Greene, in his Thomas Davis Lecture, deals with the Thurles Convention of 1887 when the IRB took over one part of the organisation and the Catholic clergy (led by a Father John Scanlon, who was a Clareman and for that reason as well as for others was strongly supported by Cusack in the *Celtic Times*) went to another place with a minority of delegates and promised to set up a rival Association pledged to support the National League. David Greene writes:

The reaction was swift and devastating; both Archbishop Croke and *The Freeman's Journal* denounced the action of the Thurles majority and, in the reconstruction which followed, the physical force men lost most of their positions of influence. Even after this purge there was a lingering suspicion that the old Fenian anti-clericalism was the hidden hand behind the GAA; two years later we find Archbishop Walsh saying: "I am fully aware that efforts have been made in some parts of Ireland to engraft upon the Gaelic Athletic Asssociation a secret society of a political nature. This fully explains what has been noticed in several districts — the scarcely-concealed hostility of certain branches of the Athletic Association to the national leaders and to Mr Parnell's constitutional movement generally." He went on to say that he suspected that British agitators were at work, but that was too much even for a reconstructed Central Council, who rejected the statement as ridiculous. It is, in fact, improbable that the IRB had any coherent plan of this kind; what had happened was that the GAA had come to embrace people of every shade of nationalist opinion, so that, even when the general direction of the movement passed into more sober hands, the physical force men continued to be well represented among the rank and file. These latter may have been luke-warm in their allegiance to Parnell in his constitutional days, but there was little doubt of their loyalty to him towards the end of his career, and two thousand of them marched in his funeral, with draped hurling sticks.

All of this is of the utmost importance to anyone who has the interests of the GAA at heart, at a time when the national question (which is shorthand for you-all-know-what) seems to be moving from the last botched-up damn good bargain to something different and, one hopes, something which will guarantee a coming together rather than a splitting of all religious, political and other groupings on the whole island: not forgetting the minority to which I myself belong.

And if all or any of the foregoing comes as a surprise to you, perhaps that indicates a need for a general work on the GAA's background, pen pictures of the various major figures involved and extracts from newspapers and periodicals of the time giving contemporary views on important happenings and decisions. Marcus de Búrca has done the important and necessary spadework, but his book is an official view (despite being described as "A History") and what I have in mind would be free of the "on the one hand this, but on the other hand that" style which cannot be avoided when one is supervised by an official committee.

As an example of what I mean, and as we have touched on politics and hinted at national reconciliation, allow me to direct your attention to the role of the GAA in post-Civil-War Ireland. That tragic and vicious conflict was perhaps even more savage in Kerry than anywhere else I know of. When I hear people bleating about the nice, clean, well-behaved wars we had in this island before the present savagery in the North disgraced our good names (particularly when the bleating takes place in honour of Michael Collins, at Béal na Bláth), I feel like taking the speaker by the ear and leading him to Ballyseedy, near Tralee.

All the more interesting then, to read in *The Kerryman* of 10 February, 1924, under the heading "Ex-Internees v. Kerry", the following:

Whatever may be the result of the match between the ex-internees and the Munster champions, it must be admitted that the former are making a decent effort to give a creditable display. Every day during the past week the thud of a football can be heard in the Sportsfield, and the early morning hours are devoted to walking exercises; so that, all things taken into consideration, it will be admitted that the ex-internees are fully determined to pull the laurels from the brows of the Kerry team.

The match was a disappointment. It was played on a flooded pitch and "was somewhat marred by a large number of fouls, the referee being kept pretty busy. On the whole there was not much to choose between the teams but the Munster champions were the more dangerous."

It was a start, and not a bad one either when one considers that both teams contained men who had been engaged in taking more lethal pot-shots at their opponents a short time previously. At the County Convention it was decided to play a second match between the teams and on 23rd of March *The Kerryman* reported:

Sunday's return match between the ex-internees and the Kerry team resulted in an overwhelming victory for the former, and placed them as undoubtedly the better team. With the exception of Con Brosnan and Phil Sullivan the majority of the County team seemed to be in a parlous condition. In connection with the match it was fought out in a fine sporting spirit which reflected the utmost credit on both combinations.

I do not wish to moralise but it seems to me that it is far more important for the GAA to continue to be a meeting-place for Irishmen and women, of all political and religious persuasions and of none, who wish to play or support gaelic games, than to strike attitudes on issues that seem to change from decade to decade. This applies particularly to the central and constant issue which was stitched into the GAA from its foundation, despite all the efforts to run away from it or turn a blind eye to it. In his book *Irish Nationalism*, Seán Cronin wrote: "The GAA is more than an athletic Association: it is a declaration of national faith and it is very strong in Nationalist Ulster."

This issue is central to all the furore about political, non-political and party political resolutions. It does not mean that there is no room in the GAA for those who do not believe Cronin's thesis, or who would wish matters to be different. What it does mean is that the GAA will have to contain the Provo, the Garda Síochána who plays on the same team but who may have to arrest him, the bank clerk who thinks all politics are boring, the Northern Nationalist who wants more attention focused on British Army harassment, the Munster anti-Nationalist who believes all such stories are Provo propaganda but who admits to getting the vapours when he hears the rattle of an Easter Lily box . . . it will have to contain them all, and many more diverse elements, and trim all their views so as to keep the ship on an even keel in rough seas.

It should also beware of prophets, my good self included, who claim to see what the future holds for the

North very clearly. In August 1969 in London, Dr Conor Cruise O'Brien, who would not be offended to be called "an expert on Northern Ireland", delivered the following prophecy: "The numbers of the IRA have been exaggerated beyond all measure. It is still very small with very little effective power and it would be wise to cast aside any ideas of it being a real major force capable of anything but exacerbating the situation by statements."

All this seems to put Earnán de Blaghd's plans for the GAA in the North into a distant cloud cuckoo-land, but I would not be too sure. If the GAA survives, it will have to deal with any new situation that comes about and may find itself across a table from Harold McCusker, for instance, who sees the GAA as the Catholic equivalent of the Orange Order, as he told me during a recent interview. When such a conversation takes place between equals, enjoying equal rights under whatever new arrangement eventually emerges from the smoke, Earnán de Blaghd's ideas may come in very useful indeed.

Cusack's views, as expressed in the *Celtic Times*, are also interesting:

> The GAA is non-sectarian — it is non-political in that it was not founded for political purposes. But I hold that every Irish movement which is supported by a large section of the robust manhood of the nation is, to a certain extent, political. . . . The GAA is non-political in so far as that no man's political convictions, openly and manfully expressed, and consciously adhered to, are a bar to his entry to the ranks of hurlers. My place of business is non-political in the same sense and in no other sense. But the cry of slaves and denationalisers is never heard there. Away with that miserable subterfuge of craven cowards.

Let me conclude with a look at this complex matter from an unusual angle. It concerns a meeting of subversives (then called an illegal organisation) from all over

Ireland, which was held in Dublin in early August 1936. It was convened to discuss the establishment of that most elusive of political aims, the Irish Republic. Among those present was Seán MacBride and, the man who told me the story, Máirtín O Cadhain.

The meeting was tense and fairly acrimonious and dragged on until a late hour on Saturday, when it was decided to re-assemble early on Sunday morning to try and reach some conclusion. This was done but after a couple of hours the mood of the meeting changed. Most of the delegates, particularly those from Mayo and Kerry who had been full of fight the previous night, fell silent and became restless; shuffling their feet and stealing furtive glances at their watches.

Seán MacBride, who was holding forth on various aspects of the matter in question, noticed this and whispered to Máirtín, who was beside him, "What's the matter, Máirtín? Is something wrong?"

Máirtín whispered back that there was nothing wrong but that Kerry were playing Mayo in the All-Ireland football semi-final later that afternoon, and that most of the delegates wanted the meeting adjourned to a later date to enable them to get down to Roscommon in time to see it.

"I see," said MacBride. "So a game of football is more important than the future of the Irish Republic?"

Máirtín O Cadhain's comment was, "I knew then that he would never do any good in politics because he did not understand Ireland."

At the GAA Congress in 1924, the President, Dan McCarthy, said that if a plebiscite was held among players of hurling and football the Ban on foreign games would go. It took them another forty-six years to agree to a plebiscite of members, which swept away the Ban. All the Belfast Congress in 1971 had to do was to declare it dead officially. The proceeding lasted less than four minutes.

Much has been made of this democratic decision and of its acceptance by those in positions of authority who were in favour of retaining the Ban. The fact is that the GAA had to go outside its established procedures to get the result the overwhelmingly majority of its members wanted. This fact is as important today as it was in 1971.

In 1938, when the GAA expelled one of its patrons, Dr Douglas Hyde, founder of the Gaelic League and President of Ireland, for attending an international soccer match in his capacity as President, most sensitive people wished the Ban would wither away of shame. That the absurd law was not merely an ass but a monstrous mule incapable of generating anything but dissension and acrimony was clear to most dispassionate observers. Still, there were those who put the other end of the telescope to the eye and pronounced that Dr Hyde, by attending the match in Dalymount Park, had expelled himself from the GAA.

This is a view put forward in *The Steadfast Rule* by Breandán Mac Lua, a book published in 1967 in a last literate effort to convince the faithful to retain the Ban. It remains the clearest expression of the pro-Ban argument and the unofficial exposition of the officially-held view: the Foreword was written by the President of the day, Séamus O Riain. To read the book now is rather like entering the caves at Mitchelstown to find men dressed in bearskins painting little pictures on the walls.

The manner of its going and the cleansing of air that followed are the aspects of the affair that remain clearest in my mind today. Personally, I found any rule or law that set one group of Irishmen to spy on another set of Irishmen, in the name of a spurious national purity, distasteful in the extreme. The Irish word *spiadóir* may have more of spit in it that the English word *spy* but the spit is there also.

But those who still exercise their powers of detection by seeking evidence of the Ban mentality in the GAA today are wasting their time, as well as betraying the very rigidity of mind they abhor in others. They would be better employed in facing up to the unwritten and far more insidious Ban which most effectively keeps Gaelic games out of many Catholic and Protestant schools. Those who control these schools were among the most vociferous critics of the other Ban, when it existed, as it prohibited their rugby, hockey and cricket-playing pupils from also playing Gaelic games – or so they seemed to say.

The Ban has long departed but no evidence of change in these schools has been forthcoming. Might it not be a good idea to organise a special competition in football and hurling for these schools, perhaps during the final term, starting immediately in Dublin city? Such a competition might not initially produce great football or hurling but it could produce some very interesting hypocrites.

Perhaps the most encouraging fact about the GAA after a hundred years is that while there is much cause for celebration there is none at all for complacency. Let us, for instance, take the state of Gaelic football. I find it most appropriate that a medical doctor has been elected President at a time when football, if it were human and his patient, would probably be in an intensive care unit.

Much as I favour the advancement of hurling it must be admitted that the resolution of the problems of football is the GAA's single most pressing problem at the moment. Tinkering with the rules has failed to eradicate the major blemishes of what is essentially an evolving game: which is not to say that it cannot evolve into a most attractive and exciting one for players and spectators alike.

This is not the place for a deep analysis of this perennial problem but it would make for a healthy start if the GAA, like the alcoholic, were to admit publicly and sincerely that the problem exists and that Gaelic football may not survive without immediate help. Once it has got the rules in order it can then tackle the equally important problem of standards of refereeing and interpretation of the rules.

And above all else, those who control the GAA's affairs must try to differentiate between genuine constructive criticism, from those who wish the Association a long and improved life, and the crepitations of the Humpty McDumptys who, apart from being little squalls in search of teacups, are very often second-division mice attempting to be first-division rats – and failing.

And for God's sake, will the GAA. . . .

Inside the sanest of us there is a wee preacher struggling to get out, and before I don my biretta and leap into the pulpit I shall tell you what the GAA is really all about; and give myself two minutes to escape.

After much consideration I have come to the conclusion that the GAA is really all about Bill Doonan heading for Monte Casino. Bill was a member of a family of travellers that settled in Cavan and he was a natural footballer. He was also a wayward Paddy and having joined the Army, and been trained as a radio operator, he itched for action in the real war that raged in Europe and elsewhere at the time. Bill deserted, crossed the Border and joined the British Army.

In the autumn of 1943 the war in Southern Italy raged and Bill Doonan was radio operator with his unit. One Sunday afternoon in September he was no longer to be seen. He vanished as if the ground had swallowed him. It was considered unlikely that he had been shot as there was a lull in the hostilities at the time. It was a mystery.

A search was mounted and they found him at last. Even when they did they found it difficult to attract his attention. He was up a tree on the side of a steep hill and seemed to be in a trance. And in a way he was, for after much effort and experimentation, Private Doonan had eventually homed in on the commentary of the second half of the All-Ireland football final between Roscommon and Cavan from Croke Park.

He was too indispensable to be court-martialled and survived the war to play soccer for a year with Lincoln City and afterwards win two All-Irelands with Cavan; one in the Polo Grounds, New York in 1947 and another in Croke Park the following year.

If anyone ever asks you what the GAA is all about just think of Bill Doonan, the wanderer, on the side of that hill, in the middle of a World War . . . at home.